Supernat

by

Phillip Rich

Ekklisia Prophetic Apostolic Ministries, Inc.

Published by Ekklisia Ministries
Copyright 2000 A. D.

All rights reserved under International Copyright law. No part of this publication may be reproduced, stored in a retrieval system, or transmitted, in whole or in part, in any form or by any means, electronic, mechanical, photocopying, recording or otherwise, without the prior express consent of the publisher. All scripture is the Kings James Version unless otherwise stated. All rights reserved.

Take note that the name satan is not capitalized. We choose not to acknowledge him, even to the point of violating grammatical rules

ACKNOWLEDGMENTS

This book is a fulfillment of a word that God gave me back in 1985 as the Lord began to unveil the material and the entire outline to the book you are now holding in your hands. Truly to God be all the glory for this precious information that He has revealed in these pages.

Special thanks is also given to my wife, Connie, whose prayers and support have kept me going all these years. And to my children, Kisha, Stan, Rachel, Ryan, Chris, and Amber

And to my Mother, Dorothy Wall, and my step Dad, Harold Wall, who both pray for me non-stop day by day.

Acknowledgment is also given to Pastor Jeff Johns and White Horse Christian Center in West Lafayette, Indiana, for their constant vigil of prayer for our family and ministry.

And, of course, a special thanks to our prayer partners and supporters whose names are in the Lamb's Book of Life. May God reward you richly for your labor of love toward us.

TABLE OF CONTENTS

1. Introduction…………………….......………1

2. The Fourfold Operational Process………...9

3. The Ministry of Supernatural Prayer.........22

4. Overcoming Hindrances........……………30

5. Added Benefits of Supernatural Prayer….42

6. Supernatural Prayer Activates the Gifts.....55

7. Gateway to the Supernatural………........67

8. The Gift That Grows and Grows………..75

9. Conclusion……………...…………………86

INTRODUCTION

Several years ago, as I was pastoring a church in the small town of Lockney, Texas, I became extremely hungry to be used by God in a mighty way. I craved the anointing and the power of God, the presence of God. I wanted the works of God that I had read about in the Gospels and the book of Acts. I knew there was an anointing of supernatural power that I had not yet tapped into. I had laid hands on a few sick folks and they had received their healings. I had prophesied a little. I had seen some people get saved, some people get filled with the Holy Spirit and some other good things happened. But I had not seen what my heart desired to see. I desired to see supernatural signs and wonders. I desired to see God as big as I knew He really was. I yearned for God to operate in His fullness through my life and through the ministry and I wanted to see the masses come to a saving knowledge of Jesus as Savior and Lord.

Matthew 7:7: *"Ask and it will be given unto you. Seek and you shall find. Knock and the door will be opened unto you."*

So I began to seek the Lord. I began to say, "Lord, there has to be a key to this. I know there is something that I'm not quite getting." So I did a lot of fasting, praying and waiting on God. Many nights I would stay up all night in the church all by myself. I would lie down across the platform on my face and would weep and cry before the Lord. I would say, "Lord there has to be an answer. I know there is. You've just got to tell me, you've got to teach me these hidden things." And as I was seeking the Lord, I didn't realize that God was already working. He was giving me the answer to my questions.

The Lord began by giving to me different teachings from many different ministries. Different people would begin to share a little tasty tidbit here and a morsel there. But the one thing that was brought up repeatedly, by people who were flowing in some awesome anointings, was the great need to pray in the Spirit. They all agreed that there is a great need to yield to, what I call, *"supernatural prayer"*. There is great power to be received through praying in the Spirit.

NATURAL VERSUS SUPERNATURAL PRAYER

Everyone will agree that prayer is a vehicle that releases our faith to God. One can have faith in his heart, but that faith has to be released through your words, your prayers, and even through your actions. There are many different types of prayer just as there are many different types of vehicles. One of the main types of prayer is prayer in tongues, which is prayer in, of and through the Holy Spirit. The other main type of prayer is prayer in our natural vernacular, with our own articulate speech. Your natural prayer language is the language that you normally use, whether you speak Spanish, English, Japanese, or whatever you normally speak. But when you pray in tongues, you pray in a language that is a supernatural language that is given to you by God.

The natural vehicle of prayer can be likened to the old horse and buggy. It will get you where you need to go. Our normal articulate prayer is like speech, with your own mind, your own understanding, your own reasoning. It is like carrying your faith in the level of the horse and buggy. Prayer in the spirit, which is supernatural, is likened unto carrying your prayers in a jet airplane. They may both get you there. That horse and buggy is going to get you there eventually, but if you really want to go in style you want to use the best.

1 Corinthians 2:14: *"Spiritual things are to be spiritually understood... And that which is of the flesh is flesh and that which is of the Spirit is Spirit."*

The last few years there has been a growing desire among God's people in the arena of prayer and intercession. This desire is resulting in an increased awareness of the Holy Spirit and His ministry in and through the individual who is born of the Spirit and called according to His purpose.

1 Corinthians 14:14, A.V.: *"For if I pray in an unknown tongue my spirit (not my head or my own thinking or my own desire) by the Holy Spirit within me prays."* K.J. version says, *"..If I pray in an unknown tongue, my spirit prays."*

It doesn't say, "...my natural man prays." It says,"...my spirit prays." There is a big difference between my natural man doing the praying and my spirit man doing the praying.

1 Corinthians 14:14, A.V.: *"For if I pray in an unknown tongue my spirit by the Holy Spirit within me prays but my mind is unproductive, it bears no fruit and helps nobody*

God's Word is saying that if I try to pray to God out of my natural mind then I am operating on a level much lower than I could be. It will still be effective, but I am limiting the effectiveness of my praying if I am praying according to my own natural thinking and my own natural desires.

In contrast, if I pray in the Spirit, the supernatural Holy Spirit (dwelling inside of my supernatural spirit) gives me the utterance, the language, the words that I speak out. In other words, the Holy Spirit gives me the prayer that I speak out. By doing that, I enter into the supernatural realm. I am no longer operating on a natural level, but on a supernatural level.

1 Corinthians 14:15, A.V.: *"Then what am I to do? I will pray with my spirit by the Holy Spirit that is within me, but I will also pray intelligently with my mind and with my own understanding. I will sing*

with my spirit by the Holy Spirit that is within me. But I will also sing intelligently with my mind and with my own understanding also."
1 Corinthians 14:15, K.J.: *"What is it then? I will pray with the spirit, and I will pray with the understanding also: I will sing with the spirit, and I will sing with the understanding also."*

Notice here that Paul said that I have a choice. He said, *"I will..."*. It is an act of my will. I make the choice to pray and I make the choice how to pray. I am in control of my prayer life.

Also, notice that Paul said he willed to pray *"with"* the Spirit. That means the Holy Spirit and I are involved together. When I pray *with* the Holy Ghost, I enter into a *"koinonea"* (a direct contact, a working relationship, a fellowship) with the Holy Spirit of God.

NATURAL VERSUS SUPERNATURAL

1 Corinthians 15:44: *"It is sown a natural body, It is raised a spiritual body."*

Paul said in 1 Corinthians 14:15, *"...I will pray with the understanding also."* In other words, Paul said that he also would pray with his natural mind, understanding what he was praying. There is a natural you and there is a spiritual you.

1 Thessalonians 5:23: *"I pray that your whole spirit, soul and body will be preserved blameless until the coming of the Lord Jesus Christ."*

You are not just a human fleshly person. You are a spirit-man, created by God, who possesses a soul (which is your mind, will and emotions) and who lives in a physical body. You are first a spirit person. Your spiritual side is your highest level of being. That is the side of you that comes in direct contact with God. Your soul comes into direct contact with the realm of reasons, thought, feelings and emotions. Your physical body comes into contact with the natural realm, the physical things of this earth.

We need to transcend the natural fleshly things, even the carnal, mental reasoning, in order to ascend into the supernatural spiritual realm. We can do that only by operating out of our spirit man, by praying in the Spirit. When we pray in the Spirit, we move into a higher realm, the supernatural realm.

There are two basic parts found in the natural man. There is the fleshly part, which consists of natural, physical aspects of a man and his basic natural, physical needs. The other part of the natural man is the mind, which consists of natural reasoning, thinking and decision-making. While the natural man is in contact with the natural, physical things, the spiritual man is in direct contact with the spiritual realm. If you are born again, your spiritual man s in direct contact with God. If you're not born again, your spirit is in direct contact with the other spirit, the devil.

NATURAL PRAYER VERSUS SUPERNATURAL PRAYER

Natural prayer is man trying to pray what he desires and what he can reason out with his natural thinking.

Supernatural prayer is man's spirit praying what the Holy Spirit within him is desiring, bypassing the natural desires and the carnal thinking. Praying what the Holy Spirit desires *always* results in praying the mind of God and God's perfect will. So, supernatural prayer is man's spirit praying by the Holy Spirit in him that which the Spirit of God desires, thereby always praying God's perfect will for every situation.

SUPERNATURAL PRAYER IS PRAYING GOD'S PERFECT WILL

Romans 8:26 & 27: *"Likewise the Spirit Himself helpeth our infirmities: for we know not what we should pray for as we ought: but the Spirit itself maketh intercession for us with groanings which cannot be uttered. And he that searcheth the hearts knoweth what is the mind of the Spirit, because he maketh intercession for the saints according to the will of God."*

When you pray in the Spirit, you are always praying 100% God's will in every situation. The *"infirmities"* mentioned in Romans 8:26 is that we don't always know God's will for a particular situation. The Holy Spirit always knows.

1 John 5:14 & 15, *"And this is the confidence that we have in Him, that, if we ask anything according to His will, He heareth us: And if we know that He hear us, whatsoever we ask, we know that we have the petitions that we desired of Him."*

The Holy Spirit will always pray the will of God. We know that God's Word is also His will. But there are times when the Word is silent in areas where we need to know the will of God. For example, the Word of God will not tell you whether you should live in Indiana or Ohio or somewhere else. You can't find the answer for that particular question in the Bible but you can pray in the Spirit and get God's will on it. You can allow the Spirit of God to intercede through you, praying God's perfect plan for your life.

In other words, we *know* that if we are going to pray in the Holy Ghost, that's going to be one prayer that *will* be answered. If you want to always get your prayers answered, simply pray in the Spirit.

REVELATION BRINGS UTILIZATION

Until you get a fresh revelation of something, you will never be able to do it. Until you get a revelation of salvation, you'll never receive

salvation. Until you have a revelation of the blessings of giving and receiving, you'll never enter into it. Until you have a revelation that God wants to use His children, you'll never be the vessel that God is using. And, until you get a fresh revelation and God makes it real to you about the infilling of the Holy Spirit, you'll never speak in tongues and you'll never have a prayer language that is fully activated.

1 Corinthians 2:11: *"For what man knoweth the things of a man, save the spirit of man which is in him? even so the things of God knoweth no man, but the Spirit of God. Now we have received, not the spirit of the world, but the spirit which is of God; that we might know the things that are freely given to us of God."*

UNVEILING THE SECRETS OF SUPERNATURAL PRAYER

One of the most exciting journeys that I have been on in the last few years is the area of prayer in the Spirit. It has been one of the most exciting, fulfilling and powerful endeavors of my whole life. The study and resulting revelation of supernatural prayer has changed my life.

In the chapters to come we shall unfold the different avenues as well as the different blessings involved in prayer in the Spirit. We will begin to see that there are things untapped by God's people that are available and were meant for us to possess from the very beginning. But now, as we are beginning to see, the hidden things are being revealed to us by the Apostles and the Prophets, as part of the plan that Paul prophesied. They have been kept hidden from the foundation, but now are being revealed because it is now time for us to know. It is time for us to enter into the secret things that God has destined for the church.

Ephesians 3:1-5: *"For this cause I Paul, the prisoner of Jesus Christ for you Gentiles, If ye have heard of the dispensation of the grace of God which is given to me to you-ward: How that by revelation he made known unto me the mystery; (as I wrote afore in few words, Whereby, when ye read, ye may understand my knowledge in the mystery of Christ) Which in other ages was not made known unto the sons of men, as it is now revealed unto his holy apostles and prophets by the Spirit;"*

Deuteronomy 29:29: *"The secret things belong unto the Lord our God, but the things which are revealed, unveiled, belong to us (we get title deed to them) and to our children forever that we might do all the words of this law."*

Amplified Bible?

THE FOURFOLD OPERATIONAL PROCESS

Ephesians 3:20: *"Now unto him that is able to do exceeding abundantly above all that we ask or think, according to the power* (the Greek word for "power" is "dunamis" - where we get the word "dynamo") ***that is inside of you."***

The word, *"dynamo"* does not describe a one time explosion that is quickly spent. It does describe a constant flow, a constant explosion of anointing, a constant explosion of power. *According* to the release of power and energy that is inside of you.

The question is, *"Have you received your dynamo yet?"* The gift of the dynamo. God's atomic generator in your spirit. In this chapter, we will be looking at scriptures on how to operate your dynamo. How to get it going, how to release it, how to turn it on. God places it in our life for a purpose. He doesn't want it to just sit there inactive, collecting dust.

Acts 1:8: *"And ye shall receive <u>power</u> ("dynamo") **after** ("after") that the Holy Ghost has come upon you."*

Notice that the Bible does not say *"before the Holy Ghost has come upon you."* Why not? Because the generator has to generate before there's any power.

In Acts 19:2: *"And He said unto them, <u>Have ye received the Holy Ghost</u> since ye believed? And they said unto him, We have not so much as heard whether there be any Holy Ghost."*

The phrase, *"Have ye received the Holy Ghost"*, in Greek makes reference to the *"pneuma hagiaan"* which means "that gift by the Holy Ghost." Have you received the gift that comes from the Holy Ghost? Have you received your dynamo yet? Many Christians do not even know that there is such a thing as a dynamo, just like they answered in Acts 19:2. But after they heard about it, faith was released in their heart to receive it. Verse six tells us that Paul laid his hands on them and they received the Holy Ghost and began to speak with other tongues.

Acts 2:38: *"..., Repent, and be baptized every one of you in the Name of Jesus Christ for the remission of sins, and you shall receive the gift of the Holy Ghost."*

You shall receive the gift that comes from the Holy Ghost, by the Holy Ghost. It is placed inside of you after you have received it, after you have taken it and embraced it as your own.

There have been many misconceptions about what the Baptism of the Holy Ghost is. Many people are so confused that they have thrown the baby out with the bath water. They've thrown tongues out the door. Being filled with the Holy ghost is not just going to church every once in a while and in a moment of heightened emotion you speak a few syllables. That is not being filled with the Holy Ghost and that is not what it's for. The main purpose of it is the prayer language. Why do we need to speak in tongues? What is the purpose, the reason for speaking in tongues? It is the prayer language that produces the power of God in our lives enabling us to do the work of God.

You don't find much teaching on this subject and when you do, it's telling you that it doesn't exist anymore. That it has been done away with. But, I still need help with my prayer life, how about you? Just like Romans 8:26 & 27 says, there are times that I don't know how to pray, or what to pray about. I might know that I'm upset or I'm stirred up about something, that there's a problem, and I don't know how to deal with it. I need a helper, a *"paraklete."* One who goes along side, one who lives in me. One who is for me, with me and in me.

PARTICIPATION PROCESS

The greatest way to get the Holy Ghost active in your life is by praying in the Spirit. You activate Him every time you pray in the Spirit. While you are praying in tongues you may not feel anything because you are actually generating power. When you release that power you'll feel plenty because it is a power stronger than electricity, much more powerful.

Acts 2:4: *"And they were all filled with the Holy Ghost, and began to speak with other tongues, as the Spirit gave them utterance."*

The Bible says basically the same thing in Acts 10:45 and Acts 19:6. These scriptures reveal to us *who* does *what*. God wants participation. He wants you to join hands with Him for a miracle. Without God you cannot, without you He will not. He chooses to use mankind. Miracles in the bible, like the parting of the Red sea would have never happened if Moses hadn't taken the rod and obeyed God. Moses had to do something or nothing would have happened. It wasn't all God, and it wasn't all Moses. It's God and man joining hands to accomplish a task and bring about the desired results.

Why would we expect it to be any different with the prayer language? If God won't do it all in other areas, why would He do it all in our prayer language? Even for me to get miracles, I've got to believe, or somebody else does. God won't just dump it on you. Somebody has to pray and believe. For me to get saved, I have to confess with my mouth the Lord Jesus and believe in my heart that God has raised Him from the dead. I have got to confess and believe before God can even save me.

Before I can get healed, I have to pray and believe or somebody else has to do it for me. It is God and man joining hands together for a miracle.

Mark 11:24: *"Whatsoever things you desire when you pray, believe that you receive and you shall have them."*

First we must realize the baptism of the Holy Ghost is intended as a gift for us and then we just receive it by faith. We believe it and then we receive it. Don't wait until you get it and then say, *"Now I believe it."* That is not faith. Faith is believing you have something before you have it in the natural. The title deed and the assurance are in your heart when you have faith.

Hebrews 11:1: *"Now faith is the substance of things hoped for, the evidence of things not seen.*

What is the *"evidence?"* It is the assurance that is in your heart. You know that you have it because you believe it. Then it manifests in the natural. So the prayer language is something we receive by faith.

Acts 2:4: *"And they were all filled with the Holy Ghost, and began to speak with other tongues as the Spirit gave the utterance."*

Who does what? What do *"they"* do? *"They"* speak. Who gives the words to be spoken? The Holy Ghost. They do the speaking and the Holy Ghost gives the utterance. Participation is the key.

Acts 10:46: *"For they heard them speak with tongues . . ."*

The Holy Ghost is not the *"them."* The people were the *"them."* *They* spoke as the *Spirit* gave the utterance.

Acts 19:6: *". . . and they spake with tongues . . ."*

There is something the Holy Spirit does and there is something we do. We can refuse to speak. God doesn't force us to do anything or He wouldn't be God. The devil is the one who forces. God leads us and we have got to participate with Him. We have got to get involved with God.

So we receive the Holy Ghost by faith and begin to speak. You might say, *"But it will sound funny."* Of course it will. Japanese sounds really funny to me. It sounds like gibberish. But it is a real language to somebody. Spanish sounds strange to me, like somebody's just making something up, but to somebody it means something. When you are talking in tongues, it may sound like gibberish to you, but it means something to somebody.

In a later chapter, we will talk about the hindrances the devil brings to keep you from praying in tongues. And that's one of them.

SANCTIFICATION PROCESS

Matthew 3:11 & 12: *"I indeed baptize you with water unto repentance: but He who cometh after me is mightier than I, whose shoes I am not even worthily to bear: He shall baptize you with the Holy Ghost, and with fire: Whose fan is in his hand, and he will throughly purge his floor, and gather his wheat into the garner; but he will burn up the chaff with unquenchable fire."*

You receive the fire baptism by praying in the Spirit long enough. We haven't seen too much fire baptizing lately. We've often seen the first step, the baptism of the Holy Ghost, but not many have experienced the second step. The second step is what really changes you. But it doesn't come by just saying a few syllables in tongues.

John G. Lake talked about how many hours he prayed in the Spirit and about what happened with the fire baptizing in his life. He said it changed his whole life and ministry. Perhaps he had been baptized in the Holy Ghost for quite a while, a number of years or whatever. But he said it was after the fire baptizing that he began to see miracles he had never dreamed of.

In Pentecostal circles we talked about tarrying services. I don't believe you have to tarry to *receive* the Holy Ghost but you ought to tarry *after* you receive the Holy Ghost. We need to tarry for hours, praying in the Spirit until the fire of the Holy Ghost begins to burn in us. It will make a change in your life, for all time and eternity.

Acts 2:3: *"And there appeared unto them cloven tongues like as to fire . . ."*

God began to fire baptize the church in the very beginning. Notice that we are not told how long they were praying in tongues. They could have been praying for hours.

I've been in services where they would have to carry somebody home praying in tongues. They had received the Gift. They got turned on. My Grandmother, for three or four days, every time she opened her mouth, all she could do was pray in tongues, after she received the Holy Ghost. She was so turned on to it, so engulfed in the Spirit. She probably could have stopped it if she wanted to, but she was so wrapped up in Jesus she wanted to keep on.

Leviticus 23:15*:* *"And ye shall count unto you from the morrow and after the Sabbath, from the day that ye brought the sheaf of the wave-offering; seven sabbaths shall there be complete*

The word *"Pentecost"* in the Hebrew means *"50th."* It refers to 50 days after Passover. In Acts 1 the bible says that Jesus, after He rose again from the grave, was with the disciples for 40 days before He was caught up. So there were ten days they prayed and waited on God, before the Holy Ghost was poured out.

Leviticus 23:16: *"Even unto the morrow after the seventh sabbath shall ye number 50 days; and ye shall offer a new meal-offering unto the Lord. Ye shall bring of your habitations two wave loaves of two-tenth deals. They shall be of fine flour. They shall be baked with leaven."*

This is the only time you will see an offering of bread baked with leaven. The measurement term *"two-tenth deals"* meant that each loaf was baked with a half a gallon of fine flour.

The fine flour represents our Lord, Jesus Christ, without any impurities. The leaven represents mankind, you and I. Guess what the fire that bakes them is. *"He shall baptize you with the Holy Ghost and Fire."*

Those loaves were placed inside an oven and engulfed (baptized) with heat and fire. There were two loaves. One represented the Gentiles and the other the Jews. God made provision for both, even way back then. The loaves were 28 inches long, 16 inches wide, and seven inches high. They weren't burnt to a crisp, either. They were cooked just right, until all the leaven was burnt out. And it left bread that tasted wonderful and it was to be eaten.

So how does that represent our lives? Jesus is the fine flour and the leaven is us, with our impurities and our problems and all of the sins in our lives. We are put together with Jesus in salvation, mixed together or joined with Him. Thus joined we are placed in the anointing of the Holy Ghost, baptized in the fire until (we are going to have to pray in tongues long enough) all the leaven was burnt out. All the selfishness, all the sin, all the self centeredness, all the carnality, . . . is burnt out.

That is the sanctification process of the Holy Spirit. We need to pray in the Holy Ghost until all the leaven is burnt out.

Romans 8:13 *"For if ye live after the flesh* (after the carnal desire. The leaven in your life is the carnal desire.) *... ye shall die . . . but if ye through the Spirit, do mortify the deeds of your body, ye shall live."*

The word *"live"* is *"zoe,"* the abundant life.

ACTIVATION PROCESS

The "activation" or energizing process involves you participating in praying in the Spirit and as a result, activating your dynamo. God will not make you pray in tongues. Your lips will not just take off going. God will not make you serve Him. You would be a robot and He does not want you to be a robot. He wants you to make a decision to serve Him because then He has got your real true love by an act of your will.

1 Corinthians 14:4: *"He that speaketh in an unknown tongue edifieth himself."*

The word *"edify"* comes from a Greek word, *"oikodome,"* which means your spiritual house. When you pray in the spirit, you are building up your spiritual house, building yourself up spiritually, charging your spirit, like you would charge a battery.

When you are charging a battery, you don't see a lot of things happening, or feel a lot of stuff happening. Have you ever charged a battery? Have you ever sat back and watched that battery jump around while it is being charged? Of course not. It just sits there doing nothing but it is charging. Only when you make a demand on that battery, at a moment of need, is there any release of power. When you hook terminals to it and turn the key and make a demand on that battery, then the power comes and you see results.

It is the same way with your spiritual life. When you pray in the Holy Ghost, you have hooked yourself up to the power of God, the Holy Spirit, and you are charging that battery.

You may not feel a thing because you are just charging. But when you pray for somebody, or when something happens that you need some power, Holy Ghost Power, then you turn on your spiritual key and you will have all the feeling you have ever wanted. Faith is the key that releases the power. Now, if there happened to be a need in your life while you're praying in the spirit, you may start feeling something then because there is being a release of the power.

[Handwritten notes at top: Principles — Tongue - Power / Holy Ghost Tongue - Holy Ghost Power / laws of power - laws of ability]

Whenever we go to the hospital to pray for someone, we first pray for long periods of time, charging our dynamo. When we get there, a demand is made on our faith and when it is released healing results. You can put demand on it when the demand is there, otherwise, just charge your battery and don't worry about whether you feel anything or not.

Jude 20: *"Building yourself up on your most holy faith, praying in the Holy Ghost."*

The word, *"building"* is the same Greek word, *oikodome*, your spiritual house, your spiritual building, your battery. When you are building it up, you're charging your battery.

2 Corinthians 13:14: *"the love of God, the grace of our Lord Jesus Christ and the communion of the Holy Ghost be with you all."*

Communion means communication, participation and activation. You can't have communion with the Holy Ghost unless you do something with Him, unless you join hands with Him. He is a person.

Mark 16:20: *"And they went forth, and preached the word everywhere, the Lord working with them, confirming the word with signs following."*

So the Holy Ghost began to confirm it as they preached the Word. If they hadn't preached the word, there would be no confirmation. There is participation, joining hands with God. You don't do it by yourself and God doesn't do it by Himself. He chooses to walk with man and join with us for the miracles. What do you think the gift of working of miracles is? It is where you work a miracle with the power of God. You do it with God's power.

Mark 16:18: *"You shall lay hands on the sick and they shall recover."*

But what if you don't lay hands on the sick? There is something you have got to do. You cannot flow in the power of God unless you are willing to participate with the Holy Ghost. And that means actively praying in tongues even when you may not feel like praying in tongues or when you don't feel spiritual. Remember that the Holy Spirit is a person, not a feeling.

[handwritten: participate w/ Him regardless of feeling]

MANIFESTATION PROCESS

The fourth step is the manifestation process. Once you have built up the stored power in the dynamo you are ready to release it at the time of need, when there is a demand for it.

1 John 5:14 & 15: *"And this is the confidence that we have in Him. That if we ask anything according to His will, he heareth us. And if we know He heareth us, we know we have the petitions we have desired of Him."*

James 4:2,3 talks about us praying amiss, and consuming it upon our own lust. That often happens when we pray out of our own minds. Then we are not praying the will of God. But if we are praying the direct word of God, then we know that we are in the will of God.

There are some things we may not find answers for in the Bible. For example, when a young man is looking for a companion . . . "Lord, should I marry this woman?" You can't find her name in the Bible, so how are you going to pray the will of God? Only when you pray in the Spirit. There are times when we need to pray about making a trip, or going to a certain place. Is that stated specifically in the Bible? NO. Then how do you pray the will of God about it? You pray in the Spirit.

Romans 8:26 & 27: *"Likewise, the Spirit also helpeth our infirmities (our weaknesses) for we know not (that is our weakness . . . we don't know how) how to pray as we ought. But the Spirit Himself maketh intercession for us with groanings that cannot be uttered (or articulated in English). And He that searcheth the hearts knoweth what is the mind of the Spirit, because he maketh intercession for the saints according to the will of God."*

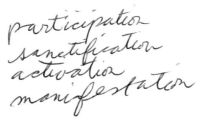

The bible says here that if I pray in tongues, I'm praying the will of God. 1 John 5:14 & 15, says if I pray God's will, I will get the petitions I have asked for. It is saying that when I pray in tongues, I *will* get an answer. I *will* receive what I am praying about. The manifestation *will* come.

There may be a time that I am praying in tongues about a loved one and not even know it, unless God reveals it to me. I may be praying about an accident that is about to happen and my praying in the spirit would stop it from happening, but my natural mind would never know it was about to happen.

CONCLUSION

You need to pray in tongues like you need to breathe. Your spirit man needs to pray in tongues like your natural man needs to breathe oxygen.

1 Corinthians 14:3: *"He that speaketh in an unknown tongue speaketh not unto men, but unto God. Howbeit in the spirit he speaketh mysteries . . . "*

"Mysteries" are those things that the natural mind doesn't know. You may all of a sudden get burdened to pray and you don't know why, so you start yielding yourself to the Holy Ghost and start participating with Him. You start speaking out the utterance He gives you. You pray until there is a release, or a joy, or a peace. You know you have received your answer when there is peace, joy, or a release inside of you.

Through spiritual prayer you change things that your natural mind would not know how to pray about. For example, you may save your loved ones from death or perhaps an accident that one of your kids may be getting ready to get into that you wouldn't know anything about or know how to stop. You couldn't pray because you couldn't know what was happening. But God knows everything. Supernatural prayer gets you into the supernatural realm where the Spirit of God is.

1 Cor. 2:4 & 5: *"And my speech and my preaching was not with enticing words of man's wisdom, but in demonstration of the Spirit and of the power. That your faith should not stand in the wisdom of men, but in the power of God."*

Paul said he didn't come to them to just preach a good message. He came to them with supernatural powers and abilities. And how could he do it?

1 Cor. 14:18 tells us he spoke in tongues more than anyone. Paul was talking about the church at Corinth. They spoke in tongues so much that Paul had to come in and say, "Now listen, when you preach and teach, would you talk in the language that people can understand? You talk in tongues so much and there's a time when you need to be understood by other people." Yet he said, "I speak in tongues more than the whole bunch of you and you are all fanatics." Later in Galatians he said, "I have come to dreams and revelations of Jesus."

Ephesians 5:17-19: *"Be ye not unwise, but understanding what the will of the Lord is. Speaking to yourself in psalms hymns and spiritual songs."*

That means singing in the Spirit. *"Singing and making melody in your heart to the Lord."* He said that's the will of God . . . for us to sing and to pray in the Spirit. And how often?

Ephesians 6:18*: "praying always . . . "*

Driving down the highway, when you go to bed at night . . . When you get up in the morning . . . You don't have to pray very loud . . . You can pray where you can hardly hear it, but you are turning on your dynamo.

I once worked in a place in Hobart, Ok., called C R Industries, where they made oil seals. I was running a press and it would get 410 degrees. I was making those oil seals, putting those parts in and taking them out just as quickly as I could. But there was so much noise from those presses and everyone stood far enough away from each other you could holler and scream and nobody would hear you or know what you were saying. I would get to singing in the Spirit and I would get to talking in tongues softly. I could do that all day long because it didn't require my mind to do it. I started having visions of people at an upcoming revival and knowing what their problem was. When I went to that revival and called them out and told them exactly what their problem was, they said that's exactly right.

You cannot pray in tongues too much. And you don't know what might be happening to your spirit or happening to someone else because you do.

THE MINISTRY OF SUPERNATURAL PRAYER

Romans 14:17: *"For the kingdom of God is not meat and drink; but righteousness, and peace, and joy in the Holy Ghost."*

It is not the things you possess in the natural realm that count, but the things you possess in the spirit. It is not the natural finances that you see that count, but it's the riches in Jesus that count for everything.

John 16:24: *"Hitherto have ye asked nothing in my name: ask, and ye shall receive, that your joy may be full."*

Your joy is full, not because you have asked, but because you have *received.* When you ask and receive, then your joy is full. So how do you believe and ask, in such a way that you will always get an answer? You can always receive what you have need of from God.

1 John 5:14 & 15: *"And this is the confidence that we have in Him, that, if we ask anything according to His will, He heareth us: And if we know that He hear us, whatsoever we ask, we know that we have the petitions that we desired of Him."*

If we ask according to His will, then we know that we have the petitions we desire of Him.

There are times when the Word of God tells us what the will of God is. We can read it. We know it is God's will for us to walk in health. We know it is God's will for us to prosper. We know it is God's will for our children to be saved, for all our loved ones to be saved. We know it is

[Handwritten annotations at top: "Sharing with God", "Communication in the realm of", "eucharist — pouring out", "+ by the means of the Holy Spirit"]

God's will for our needs to be met. We know these things from God's Word, so we can pray that way.

But there are specific things that we do not know God's Will about. We may not know His Will about things like going on vacation somewhere or choosing a mate. Maybe we don't even know how to pray when it comes to specific things concerning God's will. When it pertains to our life that there is not a thus saith the Lord on it, how do we pray? We know we need to pray the perfect will of God in order to get the answer. God is not going to leave you helpless and hopeless.

Romans 8:26: *"Likewise the Spirit also helpeth our infirmities: for we know not what we should pray for as we ought: but the Spirit itself maketh intercession for us with groanings which cannot be uttered."*

"Uttered" means spoken in your own language. So the Spirit helps our weaknesses and our inabilities because we don't know how to pray as we should.

Romans 8:27: *"And He that searcheth the hearts knoweth what is the mind of the Spirit, because He maketh intercession for the saints according to the will of God."*

The Holy Spirit enables us to pray the will of God, even when we don't know what the Will of God is.

1 Corinthians 14:14: *"For if I pray in an unknown tongue, my spirit prayeth* (not my carnal mind, not the lust of the flesh ... James 4:2,3).*"*

It is impossible to pray in the Spirit and pray a lustful, carnal prayer. Therefore we can ask the perfect will of God and receive, because we are not praying carnal, natural prayers. If my spirit prays, I am praying spiritual, supernatural prayers and supernatural prayers will bring supernatural results, supernaturally. Life begets life.

Prayer is the vehicle that releases our faith to God and the most perfect way to pray is to pray in the spirit. Let the Holy Spirit do the praying through you. Supernatural prayer is the Rolls Royce of all prayers because God is involved in helping you pray. The Helper, the Paraklete is involved.

John 16:24: *"... ask, and ye shall receive, that your joy would be full."*

Supernatural Prayer is a ministry. It is a threefold ministry. And it spells **JOY**, because you will become a receiver of what you are praying for so that your joy may be full.

J - Jesus

1 Corinthians 14:2: *"For he that speaketh in an unknown tongue speaketh not unto men, but unto God: for no man understandeth him; howbeit in the Spirit, he speaketh mysteries (hidden divine secrets)."*

There are times that your prayer is not to be known by other people. Sometimes it is to be understood only by God. Most of the time there is not to be an interpretation. Only when there are unlearned and unbelieving people nearby do they need to know what is going on. But even if you get a bunch of believers together you don't necessarily need to have an interpretation because it is a prayer to God.

1 Corinthians 14:17: *"For thou verily givest thanks well, ... "*

You are able to worship God and to thank Him in a perfect way. Have you ever desired to give God thanks and it seemed "Thank you, God" was not enough? Have you ever wanted to praise Him and "Praise You, Jesus" wasn't enough? Have you felt like you were exploding with gratitude and just couldn't get it out? But the Holy Spirit will enable you to get it out. He will enable you to express your innermost being and release it to God.

Acts 2:11 tells about the different people who were at the feast of

Pentecost and a special event took place. 120 people were in the upper room and they were all speaking in tongues at one time. Many different nationalities of people heard them speaking in tongues and they understood what they were saying. They heard them ministering to Jesus, praising God in other tongues.

Acts 13:2: *"As they ministered to the Lord, and fasted, the Holy Ghost said, Separate me Barnabas and Saul for the work whereunto I have called them."*

The Holy Ghost spoke *after* they had ministered to the Lord. Many times while we are singing in the spirit, ministering to the Lord, there will be a message in tongues come out and interpretation or prophecy. *After* we have ministered to the Lord, He will speak.

O - Others

Our ministry is for others.

Ephesians 6:18: *"Praying always with all prayer and supplication in the Spirit, and watching thereunto with all perseverance and supplication for all saints;..."*

When I pray in the spirit, there is a time when I'm praying for the saints. I may not always know whether I'm giving glory to God or whether I'm praying for others. I may not always know, but it does not always matter if I know or not. Sometimes it will be revealed to me and I will have a knowing of what I am doing.

Romans 8:27: *"because he maketh intercession for the saints according to the will of God."*

Galatians 4:19: *"My little children, of whom I travail again, till Christ be formed in you."*

Isaiah 66:8: *"When Zion travailed she brought forth her children."*

Zion is the church. When we travail with those groanings, we begin to bring forth spiritual children unto God. And once we bring them unto God, we must travail until they mature in God. It's not enough to just win someone to Jesus, but it's then our responsibility to grow them up just like in the natural. It's not enough for a young couple to bring a child into this world. That's the easy part. Then they've got to grow that child up. That takes years and discipline.

So once we bring someone to the Lord, we need to intercede in the Spirit, in the supernatural prayer language, because we don't always know exactly what they are deficient in spiritually. So how can we pray? Fathers and mothers and grandparents, you don't always know how to pray for your kids and grand kids, not like you should. You don't know the perfect prayer. You don't know what they are deficient in. What you see on the surface is not what is down deep. The problem is always covered but God knows the root. He knows the problem to the core of our being. And we can pray for our loved ones in the Spirit, as the Holy Spirit enables us, as He gives us that ability.

Those of us who have received the prayer language have the ability. We just need to learn how to yield, how to stir it up.

2 Timothy 1:6: *"Wherefore I put thee in remembrance that thou stir up the gift of God, which is in thee by the putting on of my hands."*

When Paul laid hands on believers, they received the gift of the Holy Ghost and spoke in tongues. So he said you have to stir it up. Don't let it lie dormant inside of you. You never know what you may accomplish by prayer in the Spirit.

Late one night, all of a sudden, I had a burden, a knowing that I needed to pray for somebody. It was urgent, but I didn't know what it was all about. The Holy Spirit was trying to stir me up to intercede. So I began to intercede and yield myself to the prayer language. As I began praying, it seemed like a different language, divers tongues. I got lost in the Spirit after a period of time as there was quite an unusual anointing. I prayed for one and a half or two hours but I didn't know who I was praying for. At the end of that time, there was joy and peace that came to me and I knew that everything was all right so I quit praying. And I just asked the Holy Spirit, "Who was I interceding for? What was that all about?" I could ask Him because I had *"koinonia"* with Him, I had fellowship, communion with Him. He didn't tell me until I asked. All of a sudden, I had like a mental picture, a mental spiritual picture. I saw a church in DeSoto Texas and a lady Pastor. I could see her face and I could see the front of the church. And then the picture vanished as suddenly as it came. I realized that I was interceding for her and for that church. I still didn't know what the problem was, but I knew that everything was going to be all right. That was on a Monday night. By Wednesday, I couldn't stand it anymore, I was too curious, so I called her up on the phone. I hadn't talked to her in years. I asked her, "What has been happening to you and to your church?" And I told her about the prayer time. She said, "Number 1, I've been almost deathly sick and I've been told I may have to leave the ministry. Number 2, our church has come under extreme financial bondage. We may lose the church this Friday if we don't meet the bills of the church." I told her, "Well, you're going to be all right and you're going to keep the church, too." I called her about a year or so later and I asked her how she was doing. She said, "Oh, I've never been healthier. Our church is growing and prospering." She didn't lose her church, her life or her ministry because somebody prayed in the Spirit for her.

It could have been you doing the praying. It didn't matter if it was me or somebody else. But the fact was that somebody tuned in and prayed in the Holy Ghost. There's no way I could have done it with my natural mind.

You may stop an accident from happening to one of your loved ones if you will yield to this ministry. You don't know what tomorrow holds, but the Holy Spirit does. When people say, "I don't need to talk in tongues," they don't know what they are saying. That's like saying you don't need God. Isn't He the third person of the Trinity? Hasn't He been sent to help us? You need to talk in tongues like you need to breathe. Your spiritual man needs to pray in the Spirit like your natural man needs to breathe. Isn't the Holy Spirit likened unto wind that blows? The breath, the "neshamah," of the old Testament? When God breathed into man, He breathed the breath of life, the "neshamah" of God, the Holy Ghost power, and man became a living being.

Yield to it. You may save someone's life. Don't just put it off and try to talk it away and think it's something else, think it's just a bad mood. You need to pray.

The only time you quit interceding is when you get joy and peace and you know everything is all right. Until then, you keep going. As long as you are troubled in your spirit, keep going.

Y - Yourself

Pray for yourself. Minister to yourself. We need it desperately. We need the Holy Spirit. We need help. None of us are independent from God's help.

1 Corinthians 14:4: *"He that speaketh in an unknown tongue edifieth himself."*

Remember that the word *"edifieth,"* is a Greek word, *"oikodome,"* which means to build your spiritual house, to build it up in any area that is lacking. It means to build it up until all the walls are up, all the plumbing is in, all the windows are in, all the carpeting, all the furniture, totally furnishing your spirit man. Even putting the roof on it, putting the central heating and cooling in it. When you pray in tongues, you build up your spiritual house and charge it up with supernatural energy and ability.

Jude 20: *"But ye, beloved, building up yourselves on your most holy faith, praying in the Holy Ghost."*

There are many things in life that tear us down. Even Christian brothers and sisters, who don't mean to, tear us down. Circumstances of life tear us down. The storms of this world tear us down. We continually need to be built back up. We need to edify ourselves. We need to build up the spiritual house, to charge it up with power. We need to furnish it, until every need is met.

Sometimes we don't even know what we really need. We know we are missing something, but we don't know what it is. But as we pray in the Holy Ghost, the Holy Spirit will show us what's wrong. Sometimes it is hard for us to know our own hearts, but the Spirit of God knows. He searcheth the hearts.

So, building up yourself on your most holy faith, praying in the Holy Ghost. It doesn't say praying carnal prayers. It doesn't say praying whatever came to my mind, whatever I thought I needed.

Isaiah 28:11 & 12: *"For with stammering lips and another tongue will he speak to this people. To whom he said, This is the rest wherewith ye may cause the weary to rest; and this is the refreshing."*

Isaiah prophesied that stammering lips and other tongues would be the *"rest."* He said that praying in another tongue would cause the weary (Have you ever been weary in your spiritual journey?) to rest. This brings the refreshing (have you ever needed to be refreshed?).

Isaiah went on to prophecy, *"yet they would not hear."* There are people you can teach this to and they will not listen. It goes against their carnal thinking. They can't understand it. It is too spiritual for them. The meat is too strong so they reject it.

There will be those who will not hear, but there are those who will. The hungry will hear thereof and be glad. Are you hungry for the fullness of God? Then activate your three fold ministry of supernatural prayer by praying in the Spirit.

OVERCOMING HINDRANCES TO SUPERNATURAL PRAYER

Galatians 5:7: *"Ye did run well; who did hinder you that ye should not obey the truth."*

The devil hates it when you pray in the spirit. There are five main hindrances that try to keep us from praying in the spirit. Unless we recognize them and deal with them, we will never enter into that ministry with the Holy Ghost.

Heb 12:1 & 2: *"Wherefore seeing we also are compassed about with so great a cloud of witnesses, let us lay aside every weight, and the sin which doth so easily beset us."*

There are weights, hindrances, which attempt to slow us down. There are obstacles in our way, to try to keep us from walking in the Spirit, flowing with the Spirit, having fellowship with the Spirit and/or obeying the Spirit. There are hindrances to prayer, especially to prayer in the Spirit.

THE HINDRANCE OF THE HUMAN, NATURAL, CARNAL MIND

1 Corinthians 14:14: *"For if I pray in an unknown tongue, my spirit prayeth, but my understanding is unfruitful."*

Notice that Paul said, *". . . if I pray . . ."* not, *"if I speak"* in *submit to God — but at the same time pray / resist devil* — 31

tongues. Paul is talking about prayer, a prayer language in tongues, not just speaking in tongues.

Paul said, *"if I pray in an unknown tongue . . ."* He didn't say, if I pray with my carnal mind, my natural desire, with what I could see, or what I could think was best. Paul was talking about prayer in the Spirit, praying in tongues. He said that when he prays in tongues that his spirit prays. The Amplified Bible says, *"my spirit [by the Holy Spirit within me] prays."* My spirit prays with the help of the Holy Spirit who dwells within my spirit.

1 Corinthian 6:17: ***"For he that is joined unto the Lord is one spirit."***

So you are one spirit with the Holy Spirit and He will enable your spirit to pray. He will give your spirit supernatural words that will be exactly what needs to be prayed at that time. That will result in supernatural prayer which will change whatever you or a loved one is facing. It will change things that maybe we don't even know that we are facing. But the Spirit of God knows what the problem is and what the cause of it is.

So there is a hindrance of the mind. Notice that it says, *". . . my understanding is unfruitful."* My mind is unfruitful. My mind does not know what I am saying. We want to know everything. We want to be in control of everything we say and do. And we want to be sure that it's the right thing to pray for, the thing to be said.

With our finite minds there are things we could never comprehend about the things of God or about how God works. But God knows and He has known for eons of time. We could never even imagine it, much less know to pray about it. But God already knows. So when the mind is unfruitful, that's when the push comes to shove. Because immediately, the enemy comes to work on the mind. He tells you things like this; "That's just gibberish." "There's nothing to that." "You don't even know what you're saying." "It doesn't make any sense." "You're making up words." You hear all of this stuff because your mind is unfruitful. So the old enemy wants to come along and place something in there to cause you to doubt prayer in the spirit. To keep you from praying in the Holy Ghost because it blows him apart when you do pray in the Spirit. He can't handle that.

When Spirit filled, anointed people begin to flow in the power of God the devil hasn't got a chance. Jesus never healed one sick person, never cast out one devil until after He was filled with the Holy Ghost. So the devil doesn't want you doing any of those things. "Don't pray in the Spirit!" If he can stop you, he will stop you because you are generating a power that he can't deal with, that he can't handle.

1 Corinthians 2:14: *"But the natural man receiveth not the things of the Spirit of God: for they are foolishness unto him: neither can he know them, because they are spiritually discerned."*

So your natural mind cannot understand praying in the spirit because it is in another realm. It is above the natural mind, as high as heaven is from earth.

You cannot let your mind hinder you from praying in the spirit if you desire to enter into that ministry.

Romans 8:5-7: *"For they that are after the flesh do mind the things of the flesh: But they that are after the Spirit the things of the Spirit. For to be carnally minded is death; but to be spiritually minded is life and peace. Because the carnal mind is enmity against God (warring against God): for it is not subject to the law of God neither can it be."*

Your natural mind will think about fleshly things, natural things. A spiritual mind is one that's renewed to the things of the Spirit.

If you are having a hindrance with your mind then you need to renew your mind to the Word. What does the word have to say about prayer in the spirit? You need to study the Word, not preconceived religious ideas. If you're trying to go by what you've been taught or what you've heard somewhere else, you're probably wrong about prayer in the

The Work of the Spirit who is God in the Earth & the Agent of God the Father & God the Son — Representative of God — of Father & Son — 33

This work is through the word of the Spirit

spirit. One of the things that has been taught in the past is, "Well, you must always have an interpretation."

There is a devotional tongue and there is an inspirational tongue to minister to the body. They are two separate things. We're looking at the devotional tongue now. We're not talking about the inspirational tongue that ministers to the body. The inspirational tongue, not the prayer tongue, is the one that someone needs to interpret. We've not been taught right.

Share this

1 Corinthians 14:18 & 19: *"I thank my God, I speak with tongues more that you all. Yet in the church I had rather speak five words with my understanding, that by my voice I might teach others also, that ten thousand words in an unknown tongue."*

The church at Corinth spoke in tongues all the time, the whole bunch of them. Paul went on to say that when he's in church trying to preach to you and teach you, he would rather speak to you in a language you could understand than to speak ten thousand words in tongues. That would not edify you, it would not build up your spiritual house, unless there is an interpretation. So Paul tells us that there is a devotional tongue that he uses all the time and there is a tongue that needs to be interpreted, that has a message tagged onto it.

We've been mixed up for years and because of it the devil has wracked our minds and destroyed the prayer language. He has kept us from entering into a ministry that could change us, our family, our finances, our circumstances. So we need to renew our mind to see that there is a devotional tongue and then there is a tongue of inspiration that goes to the church that needs to have an interpretation. They are separate, yet connected. Paul was involved in both of them.

Romans 12:2: *"And be not conformed to this world: but be ye transformed by the renewing of your mind, that ye may prove what is*

The work of the Holy Spirit through the word of the Holy Spirit — It takes power to do work — word — mouth

that good, and acceptable, and perfect, will of God."

So begin to renew your mind to the fact that there is such a thing as the prayer language. And that it is a ministry that you can do at all times.

Ephesians 6:18: *"Praying always with all manner of prayer and supplication in the Spirit .. ."*

Paul said he prayed in the Spirit all the time, more than all of them put together. And they were doing it so much he had to come along and say, "Now at least when you're going to preach and teach you need to be talking in a language people could understand." They would get up to make an announcement in church and want to speak in tongues. Somebody would want to give a prayer request and out comes the tongues. They said, "Well, what are we praying about?" The preacher would get up to preach and he would preach in tongues for an hour and a half. And nobody knew what he was saying.

So Paul came along, not to discredit tongues, but to give them some wisdom. He told them that if they were going to teach somebody something, at least teach them in a language they can understand. He wasn't throwing tongues out the door.

1 Corinthians 14:39: *"Forbid not to speak in tongues."*

Do not forbid people to speak in tongues, don't tell them they can't do it, that they shouldn't be doing it.

2 Corinthians 10:5: *"Casting down vain imaginations, and every high thing that exalteth itself against the knowledge of God, and bringing into captivity every thought to the obedience of Christ . . ."*

When the enemy comes against your mind, go back to the Word. When the devil comes up and says, "You can't pray in tongues. It's not scriptural. You don't even know what you're saying. It sounds like baby talk. Those are not even words." You need to cast those vain imaginations down. You need to say, "devil, shut up. I'm not listening to you." Paul said there are many voices in the world and none of them are without significance. For every tongue that comes out, somebody knows what it's saying. You may be speaking something that sounds like total gibberish but God knows every word. So does it matter how it sounds to you? Absolutely not.

There is a battle in the mind and you must renew the mind in order to be able to fight it. You need ammunition. That is what Jesus used, *"Thus sayeth the Lord, It is written."*

So renew your mind to the word of God and cast down vain imaginations and press on. Sometimes you just need to ignore the devil. It will really blow his mind that you are ignoring what he is saying to you.

THE HINDRANCE OF YOUR NATURAL CARNAL FLESH

2 Corinthians 5:7: *"For we walk by faith, not by sight (not by our senses)."*

We should walk and function as supernatural beings instead of natural beings. God has given us the Spirit, and we are to be one with Him. Paul said we were joined to the Lord by one Spirit. But we need to walk spiritually and not to follow after the carnal flesh, after what we see or what we feel of the five senses. Those things are subject to dramatic change at any moment. But God is solid, He will not change, neither will His word change. He said in Malachi 3:6, *"I am the Lord God, I change not."* Not even the least bit of change, not even a color change.
Romans 8:13: *"If ye live after the flesh, ye shall die: but if ye through the Spirit do mortify the deeds of the body, ye shall live."*

Your body does not want to pray. It especially doesn't want to pray in the Spirit. Your body wants to be entertained. It wants the easy chair. Your body wants a good movie. Your body wants something to eat. Your body wants luxury. But the Bible says that if you do not mortify the deeds of your body you will die.

If you obeyed your body and you did everything your body wanted you to do, it would kill you physically and spiritually. If you ate as much as your body wanted you to eat, if you drank anything your body wanted you to drink, if you did everything your body wanted you to do, it would kill you. There is no end to what the flesh wants. *"But if you through the spirit do mortify* (that means to totally stop, like a mortician does with someone who dies.) *the deeds of the body, ye shall live."* We've got to mortify our carnal nature and desires.

The flesh itself is not sinful. God created it. But it's the carnal desire, following after the desire of the flesh, to do whatever the flesh wants to do, that leads to death. That's the part that needs to be mortified. You've got to take authority over your flesh. If your flesh does not want to go to church, you need to say, "We are going to church anyway." When your flesh says, "I don't want to get up to pray," you need to get up and pray anyway. Your flesh says, "Don't give any money in the offering because after church I want to go to the ice cream place and get a big sundae." You need to say, "Shut up flesh! I am putting the money in the offering plate."

Your flesh does not want to pray in the spirit. The flesh is against anything that is spiritual because there is not enough gratification in it. There is not enough physical pleasure in spiritual things. The flesh wants pleasure for the moment. The Spirit of God inside of you and your spirit says, "I can pray and receive spiritual gratification that may come later." The flesh wants it right now.

And the Bible says if you follow after that type of gratification, you will die two different deaths, both physical and spiritual. But if you mortify the body you will live two different lives, your spiritual life and your physical life, the *"Zoe,"* which is the God-kind of life. Which means that you will receive physical gratification anyway, just not right at the moment.

Your flesh is just going to throw a big tantrum if it doesn't get fed when it wants to be fed. When it gets tired, it hollers at you. When it wants entertainment, doesn't it holler at you? So we've got to learn to control the flesh because there is a battle there. The flesh would rather be gratified when we need to be doing something spiritual, or when we need to be reading the word, or we need to be praying. If we follow the flesh, we will never pray. We will not have enough time to pray. We will have time to watch tv, to eat, to sleep, to play, to gratify the flesh.

If we have time to do those things, then we have time to pray. But we have got to make a choice. Choose to either follow the Spirit or follow the flesh. If you follow the flesh, know that you will face some consequences.

Galatians 3:3: *"Are ye so foolish? Having begun in the Spirit, are ye now made perfect by the flesh?"*

Paul is asking, "You were born of the Spirit. Why do you wind up doing outward things of the flesh that have nothing to do with the Spirit?" **Romans 12:1:** *"I beseech you therefore, brethren, by the mercies of God, that ye present your body a living sacrifice, holy, acceptable unto God, which is your reasonable service."*

It is not over and above the call of duty, not extra service. It is simply *"reasonable"* service to take your body and present it unto God. Don't let it rule you or you'll never enter into prayer in the Spirit.

Take authority over your mind and take authority over your body. Those are two of the major hindrances of entering into the things of God.

THE HINDRANCE OF TIME

This hindrance is in effect when people don't seem to have enough time to pray, when they can't seem to pray very long in the Spirit or when people say, "I've never prayed very much in tongues."

1 Corinthians 14:18: *"I thank my God, I speak in tongues more than ye all."*

Ephesians 6:18: *"Praying always with all prayer and supplication in the Spirit."*

2 Thessalonians 5:17 talks about praying without ceasing.

I found out that there's only one way I can obey these scriptures and that is by praying in the Spirit. It doesn't take your natural mind. It doesn't take any thinking to pray in the Spirit. You can be driving a car and know exactly what you are doing while you are praying in the Spirit. You can operate heavy machinery and totally have your mind on what you are doing while you are praying in the Spirit. I operated machines for two years and prayed in the Spirit most of the time. And I would put out exactly the number of parts, good parts, that I was supposed to. It does not take your mind to pray in the spirit, but it takes your Spirit. That's the beautiful part about it.

So there is never any excuse that you don't have enough time for supernatural prayer. You can pray in the Spirit while you are driving down the highway or at night in your bed. If you wake up in the middle of the night you can pray in the Spirit and you don't have to pray so loud that you wake up the whole neighborhood. We get to thinking that when you pray in the Spirit you have to do it loud but you don't. You can pray quietly under your breath, where no one can tell you're doing anything. When you get up in the morning, you can be praying in the Spirit while you're doing your hair, while you're fixing your face. Talk about a time saver!

Ephesians 5:16 & 17: *"Redeeming the time, because the days are evil. Wherefore be ye not unwise, but understanding what the will of the Lord* *is."*

Ephesians 5:19: *"Speaking to yourselves in psalms, and hymns and spiritual songs, singing and making melody in your heart to the Lord . . ."*

There's no better way to redeem the time than praying and singing in the Spirit. We should not have idle time. The time's too short. Jesus is coming back very soon and there's still too much to be prayed about. So redeem the time by praying in the Spirit. And don't let the enemy tell you that you don't have time to pray. It's beautiful when you can have a quiet time for prayer, but if for some reason you don't get it, build yourself up by praying in the Holy Ghost. Get the job done anyway.

THE HINDRANCE OF THE LACK OF PATIENCE

James 1:3 & 4: *"Knowing this, that the trying of your faith worketh patience. But let patience have her perfect work, that ye may be perfect and entire, wanting nothing."*

If you will continue patiently to pray in the Spirit, day in and day out, you will see results. The first results will be a dramatic change in you. Then you will notice a change in circumstances and in the lives of other people.

1 Corinthians 2:13: *"Which things also we speak, not in the words which man's wisdom teacheth, but which the Holy Ghost teacheth; comparing spiritual things with spiritual."*

The Holy Ghost gives the right words to speak. He gives you words that fit the circumstance you are in at the moment. If you'll be patient and continue to speak those things out you will see the manifestation you desire. God knows what you need. All you can see is the surface but God sees the root. God knows the cause of the problem. You may think you know what the problem is but you don't know how to change it. God does. That's one reason why prayer in the spirit is so vital.

THE HINDRANCE OF PERSECUTION

You'll see persecution on every side. You may hear messages preached by people who mean well but who teach that tongues is not for us today, or that it is just an emotion thing, or that it went out with the apostles. Nowhere in the Word of God does it say that supernatural prayer went out with the apostles. One of the passages of scripture they use is 1 Corinthians 13:8-10, *"Charity never faileth: but whether there be prophecies, they shall fail; whether there be tongues, they shall cease; whether there be knowledge, it shall vanish away. For we know in part, and we prophesy in part. But when that which is perfect is come, then that which is in part shall be done away."* When knowledge ceases, there will be no more universities. Today there are universities springing up everywhere. We know that the perfect age has not come yet. But you hear messages like that. They pluck scriptures out of context instead of reading the whole chapter. When you read the whole context it's not saying the gifts of the Spirit are done away with. It says that they need to be decent and in order. And it gives love as the means of regulation.

Paul never quit flowing in the gifts of the Spirit and the gifts of the Spirit have never stopped. They have slowed up in places because people wouldn't receive it and they didn't know the Word. So they rejected the Word. When people reject the Word, the Holy Spirit won't be anywhere around. From the time of the book of Acts until now, people have always spoken in tongues somewhere. It has never stopped because the Holy Spirit has never left us.

John 14:16: *"And I will pray the Father, and He shall give you another Comforter, that he may abide with you forever."*

He will never leave you or forsake you. He is with you right now and forever.

Galatians 4:29: *"But as then he that was borne of the flesh persecuted him that was born after the Spirit, even so it is now."*

Your flesh will persecute you. Your natural mind will persecute you. People will persecute you. They will persecute you just because you speak in tongues. "Oh, you go to that holy roller church that talks in tongues." You'll hear things like that because the devil will do anything he can do to keep you from talking in tongues. There will be persecutions from within and persecution from without.

There will be times when you speak in tongues in church that some people don't like it. Many times, it is because they don't understand. Many Christians will go so far as to say that speaking in tongues is of the devil. If we listen to those lies, they will hinder us from praying in the Spirit. We sometimes allow persecution to affect us because these are good Christian people who are saying these things. There are good Christian people who are sincere but they are sincerely wrong.

We are to bless those who persecute us, pray for those who spitefully use us. Persecution will come. Jesus taught us in Matthew 5:10 & 11 that if they persecuted Jesus, they are going to persecute us. If they persecuted the prophets before us, we will be persecuted for our faith.

ADDED BENEFITS OF SUPERNATURAL PRAYER

There are five basic special benefits that come from prayer in the Spirit. I don't mean praying in tongues just every now and then but when you do it for a length of time. When you are involved in serious prayer in the Spirit, something happens, something explosive takes place in your life.

Acts 1:8 & 9: *"But ye shall receive power after that the Holy Ghost is come upon you: and ye shall be witnesses unto me both in Jerusalem, and in all Judea, and in Samaria, and unto the uttermost part of the earth. And when He had spoken these things, while they beheld, he was taken up; and a cloud received him out of their sight."*

In this verse Jesus was speaking to His disciples during the forty days He was seen by them after the resurrection. He went to them after He was raised from the dead and spoke some things to them, gave them some instruction and encouraged them in many different ways. He told them to go and wait in Jerusalem until they are endued with power from on high. In Acts 1:8, He begins to explain about a special endowment of power that He's going to be giving to His people. An endowment of power that has never been retracted. It is still available to believers everywhere today.

It is important to notice that this was the last bit of instruction that Jesus gave to His believers. The last bit of instruction that someone gives you before they leave to go somewhere is usually the most important. It is usually a recap, a conclusion, of everything they have really been wanting you to know.

He told the disciples that they were going to receive a very special anointing of power. This word *"power"* here is a Greek word, *"dunamis."* We have in the past thought of it as being a dynamite kind of power, one that just explodes. If you were to light a stick of dynamite and throw it on the ground, if the fuse was dry enough and if it was not too old, more than likely, that thing would explode. Now, how many times would that one stick of dynamite explode? Only one time. But, that is not the kind of power Jesus was talking about.

Jesus doesn't want us to go in and have just one big explosion, one big flash in the pan and then it's over. We have no more power, no more ability, and the devil can come in to spoil us. This word, *"dunamis,"* according to the Dake's Bible, means inherent power capable of reproducing itself like a dynamo. A dynamo is like an atomic generator that constantly reproduces explosions of power on a continual basis.

Jesus was saying here that He was not going to make us a flash in the pan, one big boom and it's over with. He was saying He was going to make us into a very special *dynamo* of power. That you will have a constant explosion of power inside of you that will reproduce itself in someone else. Isn't that powerful? Talk about being a witness! He was saying that as we pray in the Spirit, we are stirring up our Holy Ghost dynamo that was given us by the Holy Ghost.

When you were filled with the Spirit of God and spoke in tongues, you received your dynamo.

Acts 19:6: *"Have you received the Holy Ghost since you believed?"*

Have you received this *dynamo* since you believed? Have you received this endowment of dynamo power? Have you received your dynamo?

Once you have received the dynamo, you have to turn the dynamo on and you have to generate it. When we pray in the Spirit and we begin to pray in tongues, what we are actually doing is, we are flipping on the switch that is attached to the dynamo. And as we flip on the switch by faith and begin to speak in other tongues, the dynamo kicks in and begins to produce a supernatural explosion of power.

What can this dynamo power do?

One of the translations talks about this dynamo power as being a supernatural ability.

2 Peter 1:3: *"According as his divine power (dunamis, dynamo) hath given unto us all things that pertain unto life and godliness, through the knowledge of him that hath called us to glory and virtue . . ."*

This scripture is saying that this supernatural dynamo, which is this word *"power"* here, has given unto us all things that pertain unto life (a natural thing) and godliness (supernatural things), through the knowledge of Him that has called us to glory and virtue.

Notice that *"through the knowledge of Him"* we are able to enter into activating the dynamo. The knowledge of the word is extremely important because it is the instruction manual for operating your dynamo. The Word is an instruction manual which teaches how to operate these supernatural abilities that God has placed into the born again believer.

There are at least five different functions of this dynamo that are operative in our lives and are stirred up as we activate, or flip the switch, through supernatural prayer.

Ephesians 3:20: *"Now unto Him that is able to do exceedingly abundantly above all that we ask or think, according to the power that worketh in us."*

Remember that the word *"power"* can be translated *"dynamo."* The more we allow the dynamo to be activated, to be stirred up, to generate power, the more the *"exceedingly abundantly above"* things begin to happen. If you get that in your spirit, it will enable you to flip the switch to your dynamo more often.

RELATIONSHIP POWER

2 Corinthians 13:14: *"The grace of the Lord Jesus Christ, and the love of God, and the communion of the Holy Ghost, be with you all. Amen."*

The communion of the Holy Ghost is one of the things that happens when you pray in the spirit. The word, *"communion,"* is *"koinonia"* in the Greek, and it means a fellowship with the Spirit, a partnership with the spirit, a participation with the Spirit. It means joining hands with the Holy Spirit, getting to know the Holy Spirit, developing a relationship that leads to partnership, a working relationship. The more you pray in the Spirit, the more you are fellowshipping with the Holy Ghost, who is living inside of you, and the more He will begin to fellowship back with you.

Words of knowledge and the other gifts of the Spirit start coming to you and spiritual sensitivity starts happening as you begin having communion with the Holy Ghost. Sensitivity comes after you have prayed enough in tongues. That is when the Holy Spirit wants to talk back to you. With the reply comes knowings, stirrings, sensitivities, and abilities that you did not have before. He wants to communicate with you. Sometimes, He communicates by giving us open visions. He communicates by enabling our eyes to see what we could not see before.

I have had many experiences of receiving from the Holy Spirit while I was praying in tongues. I learned to take a piece of paper and then pray, *"Holy Spirit, now begin to pray through me the needs of the people and reveal it to me what I am praying about. If there is anyone I need to pray for give me names, give me details, whatever is needed."* Then I would get back to praying in the Spirit.

When I pray in the Spirit, I don't always pray real loud and hard. Sometimes it is really soft, sometimes it is singing in the Spirit, or just praying softly in the Spirit. And I listen to the sensitivities and the visions and the knowings that come to me inside my heart, inside my spirit man. And while I am doing that, sometimes I see somebody's face, and I write down what that person looks like. At times I just see what color clothes they are wearing. If I see a woman in a certain place who is wearing a blue dress, I write that down. And if an impression comes to me, I write that down, perhaps someone in her family has heart problems. And later, perhaps during a church service, perhaps in the grocery store, that will come back to me by the Holy Ghost. Then I can walk over, find that woman dressed in that blue outfit, and I can tell her, *"I saw you in the Spirit. Is there a loved one you have who has heart problems?"* 99.999% of the time that *woman would say, "Yes, it's my husband," or "it's my brother," or "it's some loved one."*

They usually ask, *"But how did you know this?"* Well, I had fellowship with the Holy Ghost.

Think about this. The Holy Spirit knows everything. If we met someone who knew everything, what would be the most logical thing to do, to get to know what they know? Go fellowship with them. Go talk to them. Say, *"Tell me some things. Tell me what you know."* As you ask questions and as you fellowship with them, you will find out things you did not know. That's koinonia. We can do the same thing with the Holy Spirit while we pray in the Spirit. There is a relationship power given to you and activated by prayer in the spirit.

RESTORATION POWER

Restoration power is a power which restores the things the enemy has sought to take away from us or to take away from others.

Joel 2:25-28: *And I will restore to you the years that the locust hath eaten, the cankerworm, and the caterpillar, and the palmerworm, my* *great army which I sent among you. And ye shall eat in plenty, and be satisfied, and praise the name of the LORD your God, that hath dealt wondrously with you: and my people shall never be ashamed. And ye shall know that I [am] in the midst of Israel, and [that] I [am] the LORD your God and none else: and my people shall never be ashamed. And it shall come to pass afterward, [that] I will pour out my spirit upon all flesh; and your sons and your daughters shall prophesy, your old men shall dream dreams, your young men shall see visions . . ."*

This is speaking about an outpouring of the Holy Spirit that will be poured out upon all flesh.

Acts 2:15 & 16: "For *these are not drunken, as you suppose, as ye suppose, seeing it is but the third hour of the day. But this is that which was spoken of by the prophet Joel: And it shall come to pass in the Last Days, Saith God, I will pour out my Spirit upon all flesh:"*

Peter saw what happened with all those people speaking in tongues and he said that is what was prophesied in the book of Joel. Joel said that there is a restoration power that is connected to the receiving of this dynamo power. And I have learned that the more you activate that dynamo by praying in the spirit, the more the enemy has to restore to you what he has taken from you, even years ago.

Several years ago, while I prayed for my Grandpa, the Holy Spirit quickened to me the fact that my grandpa could be healed of a diabetic condition that he had. The Lord let me know that the enemy had taken something very precious from my Grandpa. My Grandpa enjoyed eating. He *loved* to eat. He didn't do a lot of other things that other people do, but he really enjoyed eating. He loved to have his bacon and eggs and biscuits with a lot of butter and he would take syrup and put it all over everything. Today they say something like that would be harmful for you but my Grandpa lived to be almost 95 years old and he had a strong heart. He never had any kind of problem with circulation or anything like that. He just had that one attack with diabetes.

When I was praying in the Spirit for him, the Lord revealed to me that he did not have to be that way. He showed me that it was the enemy stealing something that he enjoyed. So I began to pray for his restoration. I began to release restoration power into his body through prayer in the Spirit and through the revelation that would come, I would speak it out to restore him. This went on for a while and finally the Holy Spirit said, *"Now, thank me for it, don't ask me anymore."* And I just began to thank the Lord.

Where did all this come from? It came from the dynamo. It came from much prayer in the spirit. And I began to thank the Lord and worship him and praise Him because my Grandpa was healed of this condition.

When Grandpa went back to the doctor they said, *"We do not understand this. He can eat anything he wants. He doesn't have anything to worry about. His blood sugar is normal and his pancreas is producing the right amount of insulin. Everything is fine. Let him eat any thing he wants to."* from that time on, for the next fifteen years, my Grandpa ate anything and everything he wanted and never ever had a problem.

RESURRECTION POWER

Romans 8:11: *"But if the Spirit of Him that raised up Jesus from the dead dwell in you, he that raised up Christ* (meaning 'the anointed one and his anointing') *from the dead shall also quicken your mortal bodies* (your physical bodies) *by his Spirit that dwelleth in you."*

The phrase, *". . . his Spirit that dwelleth in you,"* does not just mean that the Spirit is *resident* there. It means the Spirit is *President* there. It means He is doing whatever He wants to do. It means that through supernatural prayer you activate His power, His dynamo, until He is active in your life, in your spirit.

Through supernatural prayer, there is a quickening power, a

resurrection power that is available. And it is available not only for you and your body, but for others that you may come into contact with or pray for. The more you pray in the spirit, the more the healing anointings will begin to operate through you.

Brother Grant Sr. would pray 6 to 8 hours in tongues before he would go into a meeting to minister to the sick. He said the more he prayed in tongues the more sick people got healed. He said there would be anointing flowing out and people would get up out of wheelchairs and off of canes and crutches. He said the most awesome healing power would manifest. He said it was always related to his prayer in tongues. The longer he prayed in tongues, the more powerful the results. The resurrection power would come forth to restore mortal, fleshly bodies.

REFRESHING POWER

Isaiah 28:11 & 12: *"For with stammering lips and another tongue will he speak to this people. To whom He said, 'This is the rest wherewith you may cause the weary to rest and this is the refreshing.' Yet they would not hear."*

In this scripture, even way back in the Old Testament, we are given a glimpse into some revelation attached to prayer in the Spirit. And, He is telling us that some people don't want to hear this revelation. I have seen that to be true. It holds true even for people who may have prayed in the Spirit before, who may know a little something about it. It is very difficult for them to hear revelation about spiritual prayer. Sometimes they just don't want to hear it. They may think they already know all about it.

But, one of the things I have discovered about God's Word is that His Word is progressive. No one knows it all. There is always more to learn. No matter how many years I have studied the Word and sat under some very powerful ministries I have seen young people and even little children astound me with revelations of the Word of God. There is no room for pride. There is no room for feeling like we've got it all. There is always more to know and the Holy Spirit is the one who reveals His Word. And He reveals God's Word to whomever He wants to, whenever He wants to. He may choose to reveal His Word to a little child, a teenager, someone living in the street, a church member or a Pastor.

My Mother has talked many times about the refreshing power of spiritual prayer. There were times when she would not know what to do and there was worry, turmoil and anxiety in her mind. Our family lived on a farm where we raised boiler chickens for Tyson's. At one point the price of boiler chickens had bottomed out and many people were losing their farms. My Dad had just bought a big diesel truck so he could haul hay and things for other farmers and that market bottomed out, too. A lot of things happened all at once that brought a lot of pressure and a feeling that there was no rest. There seemed to be no getting out from under the load.

But my Mother wouldn't give up. She began to spend more and more time praying in the Spirit. That was the only thing that would give her the rest and refreshing she needed.

Mother would tell us many times of people whose minds would be under attack, they would be under tremendous mental torment, and the only way they could get relief was through prolonged prayer in the Spirit. As they would pray in tongues, they would receive a relief from the mental torment, the worry, the anxiety or whatever mental attack the devil had attacked them with.

Many times I have laid in bed, unable to sleep. I discovered that if I would begin praying in tongues, the worries and problems would begin to disappear until I could drift off into a peaceful sleep.

There are battles in the heavenlies today. Satan tries to attack our minds with so many thoughts they seem to come to us like machine gun bullets, attacking us so fast and so furious. If we don't pray in the Spirit, we won't have a moment of peace. Not only are we to meditate on the Word, but we need prayer in the Spirit to give us the refreshing, the spiritual "R & R" that is available from God.

REVELATION POWER

1 Corinthians 14:2: *"For He that speaketh an unknown tongue speaketh not unto men, but unto God. For no man understandeth him, howbeit in the Spirit he speaketh mysteries."*

When you are praying in tongues, many times you are praying a special revelation, a special mystery, something that you know nothing or little about. But, the Holy Spirit knows it all and He will pray through you. God never prays the problem, He always prays the solution. That is why, when you tap into spiritual prayer, you will always receive the answer.

Oral Roberts has done this for years. He would pray in the Spirit about everything for Oral Roberts University. He first received the vision of O. R. U. while he was praying in the Spirit. He would pray in the Spirit and then he would stop and ask the Holy Spirit for revelation concerning what he was praying about. Then He would begin to pray in English and he would pray out what he had been praying in tongues.

1 Corinthians 14:14 & 15: *"For if I pray in an unknown tongue my spirit prayeth but my understanding is unfruitful (my mind does not know what I am praying about.). What is it then (what will I do then?). I will pray with the spirit and I will pray with the understanding also. I will sing with the spirit and I will sing with the understanding also."*

Paul was saying, "I will pray with the spirit and I will pray with the revelation, also." This is exactly what Brother Oral Roberts did for every part of his ministry. He would pray in the spirit because he knew he was bringing to the light revelation, mysteries, things only God would know.

When you pray in the spirit, God is praying through you. And He does not pray the problem. He always prays the solution. In the Bible, Jesus always prayed the solution, never the problem.

When Jesus prayed at the tomb of Lazarus, he didn't say, *"Oh, God, please raise this man. He's dead as a doornail, stuck in this tomb here. Oh Heavenly Father, if you can just see fit, please get him out of this grave."* No way. He prayed the solution. He said, *"Father I'm not saying this for your benefit but for those who are here, that they will know that you hear me when I pray."* Then he stopped. Why did He stop? So He could hear what the Father was saying to Him, the revelation. The Father must have told Jesus to command Lazarus to come out because then He said, *"Lazarus, come forth."* And, he did.

In John 17, Jesus did not pray a defeatist prayer. He didn't pray the problem. He didn't cry and whine. He didn't say, *"Oh God, you don't know how bad things are down here. Things are just falling apart."* When you read the prayers of Jesus, you will find out how the Holy Spirit prays. He always prays the solution.

When you pray God's Word, you are praying the solution. When you pray in the Spirit, you are praying God's Word. You are praying the solution, not the problem.

So there is an answer, a revelation when you pray in the Spirit. Sometimes the answer won't be revealed to you as you pray. Sometimes it will remain in the Spirit and your mind will never know it.

1 Corinthians 2:9-13: *"But, as it is written, eye has not seen nor ear has heard nor has it entered into the heart of man the things that God has prepared for them that love Him. But God hath revealed them unto us by His Spirit. For the Spirit searcheth all things, yea the deep things of God. For what man knows the things of man save the Spirit of Man that is in him. Even so the things of God knoweth no man but the Spirit of God. Now we have received not the spirit of the world but the Spirit of God that we might know the things that are freely given us by God. Which things also we speak, not in the words that man's wisdom teaches* *but the Holy Ghost teaches, comparing spiritual things with spiritual."*

Again, that word "know" is the Greek word, "ido." That we might have a vision, that we might be able to see. In Latin that word is "video." The Holy Spirit has been given to us to show us, to literally turn on a spiritual video to show us these things.

We are going to be speaking these things, not in words that man's wisdom teaches which is how you learned English, or Spanish or whatever your natural language is. The Holy Ghost teaches a special, supernatural language and He gives it to you and helps you go from utterance to utterance. In fact, the more you press in to spiritual prayer, there will be times you will enter into divers tongues, different languages.

Smith Wigglesworth said that some people read the Bible in Greek and Hebrew, but he would read it in the Holy Ghost. He said that he knew that the Holy Ghost wrote it so the Holy Ghost knows what the meaning is. He knows what He intended to say. Only the Spirit of God can reveal the Word to you. Brother Wigglesworth said he would pray in the Spirit while he was reading the Word. And he said that while he was praying in the Spirit and reading the Word the Holy Spirit would reveal the meaning of the Word.

1 Corinthians 14:14: *"If I pray in an unknown tongued my spirit prayeth but my mind is unfruitful."*

You can be reading and praying in the Spirit at the same time and neither the reading nor the praying will be hindered. It doesn't take your mind to pray in tongues. It takes your spirit. That is why it is possible for you to read your Bible while you are praying in tongues. And when you do this, great revelation of what you are reading will come to you.

REVELATION GIFTS

As you stir up the revelation power of the Word, you also stir up the revelation gifts of the Spirit. I've found that in services when I would get a revelation, perhaps a passage would come alive or the message would be so burning in my spirit, when it would come alive inside of me and it would be so revealed inside of me, I would always know that in that service the word of knowledge, the word of wisdom, and discerning of spirits would operate at a higher level than usual. With a higher level of the revelation of the Word there is also available unto us a higher level of the revelation gifts. If you don't know that, you may not activate it, but it is available to you.

There are many special benefits of supernatural prayer. As we activate the dynamo that God has given to us through prayer in the spirit we will find ourselves gaining anointings, gaining abilities that we did not have before. Or things that we had in smaller measure are now increasing into greater measure. It's happening by the power of the supernatural dynamo that's given to us by God. We need to stir it up every day. We need to pray more than ever before in the spirit.

SUPERNATURAL PRAYER ACTIVATES THE GIFTS

Scripture teaches us in John 3 that we are born again by the Spirit. We are filled with the Spirit by the Spirit (Acts 2:4). We walk in the Spirit and the fruit is the fruit of the Holy Spirit in our lives through our spirit (Galatians 5:22). There is a way for us to activate the Holy Spirit in our lives.

2 Timothy 1:6: *"... stir up the gift of God, which is in thee by the putting on of my hands."*

Remember that this was Paul, writing to Timothy. Earlier, when Paul had laid hands on him, Timothy received the gift of the Holy Ghost and spoke with tongues. Paul was telling him to stir up that gift, to activate the Holy Ghost in his life.

You, also, can activate the gift of the Holy Spirit in your life. You can activate the Holy Spirit and know things that you couldn't ordinarily know, not only things concerning today but things to come. You can know what the devil is doing, what he is actively engaged in, as well as what God is doing with his angels. There is a way that we can activate the Holy Spirit in such a way that the gift of discerning of spirits begins to operate. There's a way of activating the Holy Ghost in your life in such a way that the word of knowledge begins to get stirred up within you, that the word of wisdom begins to be activated within you. These are things that will enable you to know what's going on in the Spirit. When you know what's going on in the Spirit, you can better handle things in the natural because you can understand them.

Most people in churches today are confused about spiritual things, about what's happening in their lives, in others, in their churches, and in situations. They simply have not understood some of the truths concerning the Holy Spirit and supernatural prayer. In these last days the Holy Spirit is revealing things to the church that for years was kept hidden because our minds weren't ready for it. We just weren't ready to receive it. We weren't hungry enough.

Matthew 5:6: *"Blessed [are] they which do hunger and thirst after righteousness: for they shall be filled."*

You'll not be filled, you'll not receive the filling, *until* you hunger and thirst. There has to be a hunger and a thirst inside of you before you will reach out to God for the answers.

If I want to know something, I can ask the Holy Spirit to show me. It is that simple. I asked the Holy Spirit once, *"Why didn't I know that before?"* He said, *"You didn't ask Me."* We miss the simple things when we're not hungry enough. God wants us hungry because when we are hungry enough, we'll eat.

And, by the way, the simple things will taste delicious. The little simple things that we overlook have the most power in them and will do the most for us. They are the things that we don't see because they are too simple. We are looking for something complicated.

KOINONIA

The key to having the gifts of the spirit in operation is simply having the Holy Spirit activated in your life. It is simply you joining hands with the Holy Spirit and having *"koinonia"* (communion, fellowship, working relationship) with the Holy Spirit. In 2 Corinthians 13:14 we find 4 things involved in koinonia with the Holy Spirit.

2 Corinthians 13:14: *"May the peace [grace] of Jesus Christ, the love of God and the communion (koinonia) of the Holy Ghost be with you all."*

1. COMMUNICATION

Koinonia involves communication (talking and listening) with the Holy Spirit.

We must always remember that the Holy Spirit is a person, not an "it." He is the third person of the Trinity. He's been sent here by the Father and He is here with us right now. God the Father and the Son are in heaven and the Holy Spirit is here. And our ability to link up with Him will make all the difference in the world.

We must be willing to talk to Him in the natural and to talk to Him in the Spirit, in the prayer language. We must *participate* in communication.

2. PARTICIPATION

Koinonia involves participation. When you are participating with the Holy Spirit, you're joining hands with Him, you are asking Him to tell you what to do and to help you do it. In other words, you are asking Him to work with you. You need to communicate with Him and make yourself available to participate with Him.

3. CONTRIBUTION

Koinonia involves contribution. When you contribute something

He contributes something.

Acts 2:4: *"They spoke as the Spirit gave them the utterance."*

They all were filled with the Holy Ghost and *they* began to speak with other tongues as the Spirit gave them the utterance. *They* spoke what the Holy Spirit gave them. There was a contribution there.

Mark 16:20: *"And they went forth preaching the word, the Lord working with them, confirming the Word with signs following."*

First, they did the preaching and then they yielded themselves to the Holy Spirit and the Holy Spirit confirmed it.

I must contribute something, to give something. I must be willing to give of myself. *"Ye shall lay hands on the sick and they shall recover."* But what if I don't lay hands on the sick? What if I don't try to cast out devils with the power of God? God uses man. With God I can do all things. Without Him I can do nothing. God chooses to use man. If man refuses, then God looks for another man. He went to Abraham to cut a covenant. He went to Noah for a covenant. He went to David for a covenant. He went to Solomon for a covenant.

God is looking for someone who will contribute something. You take one step, and the Holy Spirit will take many steps. He's just waiting for us to take a step of faith. He's waiting for us to contribute something.

4. DISTRIBUTION

Acts 3:6: *"Such as I have give I thee."*

Koinonia involves distribution. I take what I have and give it out. I take the Holy Ghost power that was given to me and I give it to somebody else. I lay hands on the sick and believe that the Holy Ghost power is going to come right out of my hands and go into their body and heal them.

Romans 8:26: *"Likewise the Spirit also helpeth our infirmities for we know not how to pray as we ought."*

The word, *"know"* in Greek is *"ido."* *Ido* means to know something, to have a video, a vision, or perceiving something. Paul said that we are not seeing or knowing anything without the Holy Spirit. Then he goes on to say that the Holy Spirit ministers to us and uses us as we flow with Him in the prayer language.

Romans 8:26-28: ". . . But the Spirit Himself maketh intercession for us with groanings that cannot be uttered (cannot be spoken in our own natural language). **And He that searcheth the hearts knoweth what is the mind of the Spirit** (He has the ido, the vision. He perceives it.) **because He maketh intercession for the saints according to the will of God. And we know . . "**

We begin to know after we have koinonia with the Holy Spirit. Then, and only then, He reveals to us what we did not know before we prayed. Verse 26 says *we don't know*, verse 27 says *He Knows* then in verse 28 *we start knowing*. We start knowing *after* we've done verse 26 and 27. That begins the word of knowledge in our lives, knowing something, perceiving something that we did not know before. So the gift of the word of knowledge is activated in our lives, where we can yield to it.

1 Corinthians 2:9: *"But as it is written, eye hath not seen nor ear heard, neither has it entered into the heart of man the things which God hath prepared for them that love Him. But God hath revealed them unto us by His Spirit. For the Spirit searcheth all things, yea the deep things of God."*

Things we wouldn't ordinarily know are revealed to us by the Spirit. We cannot know things about ourselves or about others without the Holy Spirit. If someone ministers to you a word of knowledge, they do not know that by themselves. The Word of God tells us that we don't really know ourselves. You've heard people say, *"Well I've just got to go find myself."* Well, if you had God you would. The Holy Spirit will show you who you are and what you could be.

1 Corinthians 2:13: *"Which things also we speak, not in words which man's wisdom teacheth, but which the Holy Ghost teacheth, comparing spiritual things with spiritual."*

Marilyn Hickey once stated that the words that man does not teach is the prayer language. Paul is talking about a language that has not been taught to us. You can't teach the prayer language. You can teach someone how to yield to it, but you can't teach them the prayer language. They have got to receive it for themselves and speak the language the Holy Spirit gives them, not a language a person gives them. Paul is saying here that the prayer language is not a language that man has taught you but a language that the Holy Spirit has taught you. Comparing spiritual things with Spiritual.

1 Corinthians 2:14: *"But the natural man receiveth not the things of the Spirit of God. For they are foolishness unto him. Neither can he know them."*

Notice the word *"ido"* again. The natural man cannot <u>know</u> the things of the Spirit. He cannot see, perceive or understand them because they are spiritually discerned. The *ido* comes through the Holy Spirit.

1 Corinthians 2:15 & 16: *"But He that is spiritual judges all things. Yet he himself is judged of no man for who hath known the mind of the Lord that he may instruct him. But we have the mind of Christ."*

We have the mind of Christ so we can understand the things that God has already given to us. The Holy Spirit is the revealer. He reveals the *ido* to us.

1 John 2:18-20 & 25: *"Little children, it is the last time: and as ye have heard that antichrist shall come, even now there are many antichrists; whereby we know that it is the last time. They went out from us, but they were not of us; for if they had been of us, they would no doubt have continued with us: but they went out that they might be made manifest* *that they were no all of us. But you have an unction from the Holy One, and ye know all things."*

The word *"unction"* is the Greek word, *"charisma,"* meaning the gift of the Holy Ghost. We have the gift of the Holy Ghost and He is able to reveal all things to us. Even things about spirits that are of God or not of God.

1 John 2:26 & 27: *"These things have I written unto you concerning them that seduce you* **(evil spirits)***. But the anointing which ye have received of Him abideth in you, and ye need not that any man teach you: but as the same anointing teaches you of all things, and is truth, and is no lie, and even as it hath taught you, ye shall abide in Him."*

You can not teach discerning of spirits. You don't need any man to teach you discerning of spirits because that *ido* comes from the Holy Spirit. As you pray in the Spirit and yield to the gift of the Holy Ghost, He will teach you. You can have an unction from the Holy One and you can know if something is of God or of the devil. You will be able to know if there are spirits behind it because of the unction. The gift of discerning of Spirits can operate in your life as you begin to yield to the unction of the Holy Ghost. The anointing will teach you discerning of spirits. That gift inside of you, the charisma of God will teach you. You will be able to discern good and evil. You will know it.

What about the future, what about a word of wisdom? A word of wisdom is not only knowing what is going to happen, but wisdom in knowing how to handle it. God begins to tell you what is going to happen and how to handle it.

John 16:13-15: *"Howbeit when He, the Spirit of Truth, is come, He will guide you into all truth: for He shall not speak of Himself; but whatsoever He shall hear, that shall He speak (notice the word speak): and He will show you things to come. He shall glorify me: for he shall* *receive of mine, and shall shew it unto you. All things that the Father hath are mine: therefore said I, that He shall take of mine, and shall shew it unto you."*

The Holy Spirit will reveal things to you. He will show you things to come if you enter into koinonia (communion) through supernatural prayer.

When you work with someone, you get to know them. You are able to talk to them and be with them. Over a period of time you get to know them because they share things with you. You hear things about their family, and about them.

When you pray in the Spirit, The Holy Ghost is working closely with you and you are working closely with the Holy Spirit. In that close relationship He reveals things to you and begins to show you things to come. When you are in koinonia with the Holy Spirit, all things are possible and the anointing of God gets extremely strong.

1 Corinthians 14:18: *"I thank my God, I speak in tongues more than you all."*

Paul was writing to the church at Corinth. They were talking in tongues all the time. They were talking in tongues so much they didn't even want to preach in a language people could understand. They wanted to talk in tongues all the time. They wanted to even preach in tongues and nobody could understand what they were saying. If a sinner came in, he just thought they were crazy or drunk or something.

But Paul was not putting down praying in tongues. Can you imagine him speaking in tongues more than that whole bunch put together? It is no wonder that he had the revelation he did and was able to write two thirds of the new testament.

2 Corinthians 12:1: *"I will come to dreams and visions and revelations of the Lord."*

When you begin to pray in the Spirit, you will start knowing things that you don't even know how you know them. At times you might think you are crazy because you may not like what is happening, but it looks good in the natural. You might look at the circumstances and think every thing is going to work out well but down deep inside your spirit, you're starting to know something. You're starting to understand something you didn't understand before. And you just wait, because what you are feeling inside will come to pass sooner or later.

When I was 16 years old, my Dad and I were holding a revival at Oak Park Church of God, in Chicago. Another minister came in one night and started to minister to some of the people with us at the end of the service. All of a sudden my Dad knew that man was going to do something to that church that was going to tear it to pieces. So he told the Pastor, *"That man is going to destroy you and the church."* The Pastor answered, *"No, no way. This guy loves the Lord. Everything's all right, nothing's going to happen."* He laughed it off. He later had to leave that church because of that very man.

You can know things in the Spirit and you can't go by what you can see in the natural. And don't go by the gift of suspicion either. You know when it's the Spirit of God because He keeps telling you inside. The more you pray in the Spirit, the more you know it is so. You can't go by what you can see.

Remember that man looks at the outward appearance, but God looks at the heart. God knows the future. He knows your future. It may not go the way you think. If you get in the Spirit and pray in the Spirit very much and continue to seek God, you are going to know things, you're going to know the outcome. You're going to know what is really going to happen. It will be revealed to you by the Holy Spirit.

1 Corinthians 14:5: *"I would that ye all spake with tongues."*

Paul prayed in the Spirit so very much and he encouraged us to do the same thing.

1 Corinthians 14:39: *"Forbid not to speak with tongues."*

In other words, don't forbid it, do it. You need it. Paul was able to teach us about the gifts of the Spirit because he prayed much in the Holy Ghost and these things were revealed to him by the Spirit of God. He understood koinonia and he wrote about it.

When you pray in the Spirit you pray a mystery. When you speak in tongues you are speaking divine secrets and divine secrets can be interpreted by the Spirit, through the Spirit so that your mind will be fruitful.

**1 Corinthians 2:9 & 10*: "... Eye hath not seen, nor ear heard, neither have entered into the heart of man, the things which God hath prepared for them that love Him. But God hath revealed them unto us by His Spirit: for the Spirit searcheth all things, yea, even the deep things of God."*

There are mysteries that are revealed to us by God. God reveals mysteries to those who are interested enough, hungry enough. When you get hungry enough and you want to know badly enough and you yield to the Spirit, He will tell you things.

Many years ago, I was praying in the Spirit and down in my heart the desire came up to go to Hawaii and minister in song. So I just spoke out, *"One day I will be in Hawaii, I will play a bass guitar and minister for at least two weeks."* God set it up for me two years later. Two years later I was in Hawaii playing a bass guitar and I ministered there for two weeks. I went with another singing group whose bass player quit out of the blue, so they invited me and even paid for the trip. One night at the chapel service at the college the bass player was gone so I was invited up there to play for the service. There was a member of the group at that service and God spoke to his heart and he said, "That's the one." They came right to me and drafted me immediately. That summer we went through Texas, New Mexico, California and Hawaii. By my natural mind it would have been impossible. But my trip was paid for and when I came back, God had supplied a thousand dollars for my college tuition.

When you learn to yield to the Holy Spirit there is nothing that cannot be revealed to you and anything is possible. There is a church right now in Ringling, Ok., Word of Life, last time I heard it was running in excess of one hundred people in a town of five hundred. It was started by prayer in the Spirit. After two hours of prayer in the Spirit, I had a vision of a church being on a certain road and now the church is there.

You, too, can enter into the supernatural and have koinonia with God.

1 Corinthians 14:2: *"For he that speaketh in and unknown tongue speaketh not unto men but unto God. For no man understandeth him, howbeit in the Spirit he speaketh mysteries."*

The word *"mysteries"* is talking about divine secrets that only God knows. Mysteries about persons, places or things. We can enter into the interpretation and know things we have been praying.

1 Corinthians 14:13-15: *"Wherefore let him that speaketh in an unknown tongue pray that he may interpret. For if I pray in an unknown tongue my spirit prayeth but my understanding is unfruitful. What is it then, I will pray with the Spirit and I will pray with the understanding also. I will sing with the spirit and I will sing with the understanding also."*

This scripture is saying that I can yield to the Holy Spirit for an interpretation of what I am praying in the Spirit. Usually, when I pray in English, I am praying about my problems or the problems of others. But, God doesn't pray the problem. He prays the solution. Man prays the problem. That's why praying in the Spirit is so important. It is your solution.

So we can yield ourselves to the Holy Spirit to activate the interpretation to the divine mysteries of God. So that we might know those things that are freely given unto us by God, things that cannot be ordinarily known.

One night I was doing business with another minister in a town in Oklahoma. He was wanting me to enter into a business deal with him and it sounded good. I had been praying and seeking God about it and was praying in the Spirit because I didn't know how to pray. Somehow I had a little twinge inside, a feeling that something wasn't quite right. So I began to pray in the Spirit about it. Any time you have any kind of a red light inside, pray in the Spirit, the Holy Spirit can reveal to you what's going on. So I began to pray and I went to bed and woke up in the wee hours of the morning and God spoke to me so real. He told me, *"Have nothing to do with that man, because if you do, it will hurt you."* So the next day I said, *"No, I'm sorry, but I can't have anything to do with this. I'm out of it."* Later I found out what had happened and some things that were going on and I thanked God for sparing me from it.

Because of supernatural prayer, you can know things in the Spirit, and God can speak to you. After you pray in the Spirit you can just go on in peace. Go on in peace, don't worry about it because the answer doesn't always come right then. It might be later while you are sleeping, or when you get up in the early morning. Sometimes in the early morning you are more sensitive to the Spirit. Have you ever gotten up in the morning and thought something just wasn't right? Maybe even something you were about to do. When you pray in the Spirit you build yourself up and you get ready to hear God, to receive the things that God is speaking.

GATEWAY TO THE SUPERNATURAL

3 BIBLE EXAMPLES

Supernatural power results from supernatural prayer. In this chapter, we will discuss three different people from the Bible and how they began to flow in great supernatural power after they were involved in supernatural prayer.

1 Corinthians 10:11 NAS: *"Know these things happened to them as an example and they were written for our instruction upon whom the end of the ages have come."*

Romans 15:4: *"For whatever was written in earlier times was written for our instruction that through perseverance and the encouragement of the scriptures we might have hope."*

These two passages teach us that the Word of God has examples that will help us to understand the principles, the precepts or the spiritual laws of God.

Several years ago I had a firsthand opportunity to come to an understanding of the laws and the legal system we have here in America. I discovered that if a person needs to go to court for some reason, not only must they have the law to look at, but they also need to go back and find out if there was some example, if there was some court case that was similar to what they are facing. And usually if they had two or three court cases, then they could take them to court and set the precedent for that case.

The same principle applies to scripture. The spiritual laws and the principles are stated in the Word of God. But in order to give us a really strong case in the realm of the spirit, we also have bible examples contained in the scripture. Those examples show us how that law relates and how that particular principle works.

2 Corinthians 13:1 AS: *"This is the third time I am coming to you. Every fact is to be confirmed by the testimony of two or three witnesses."*

Every testimony, every law, every principle contained within God's Word needs to be backed up with Bible examples in order for us to say, *"This is a solid foundation, something that we can hold onto as truth and as something that we can say is spiritually evident for our life and situation."* We're going to look at three of these from the Bible.

PAUL

In previous chapters we have established the fact that Paul spoke in tongues quite often. Remember that he spoke in tongues more than anyone at the church of Corinth. And we have already shown that Paul was imploring the Corinthians to speak in their native tongue when they were trying to teach and preach. Paul had to come and say that there is a time to speak in tongues and there is a time that you need to speak in your own articulate speech. He did so much praying in tongues that he said he did it more than all the church at Corinth.

As a result, we see that God began to do something very powerful in the life of Paul. Here you have cause and effect. The cause was that he spoke in tongues a lot. The effect was a special anointing of miracles.

Acts 19:11 & 12 NKJ: *"Now God worked unusual miracles by the hands of Paul so that even handkerchiefs or aprons were brought from his body to the sick and the diseases left them and the evil spirits went* *out of them."*

God began to work some very special miracles (KJ reads, *"special miracles"*) through Paul because he began to stir up some anointing and he began to build himself up on his most holy faith, praying in the Holy Ghost. He began to charge his spirit for a release. When you pray in tongues, you charge your spirit for a supernatural release of power at the point of need.

PETER

Acts 2:1-4: *"When the day of Pentecost had fully come they were all with one accord in one place. And suddenly there came a sound from heaven as of a rushing mighty wind that filled the house were they were sitting. Then there appeared to them divided tongues as of fire and sat upon each of them, and they were all filled with the Holy Spirit and began to speak with other tongues as the Spirit gave them utterance."*

There was a group of individuals here who were filled with the Holy Spirit and in the first chapter we learned that Peter was one of them. It is interesting to see what Peter did next. He actually stood up and began to tell the onlookers in the streets what God was doing.

Acts 2:15 *"These men are not drunk as you suppose, as this is but the third hour of the day but this is that which was spoken of by the prophet Joel."*

In Acts 4 the Bible tells of another prayer meeting that Peter was in.

Acts 4:29 - 31: *"Now, Lord, look on their threats and grant to your servants that with all boldness they may speak your words by stretching* *out your hands to heal and that signs and wonders may be done through the name of your holy servant Jesus. And when they had prayed the place where they had assembled together was shaken and they were all filled with the Holy Spirit and they spoke the word of God with boldness."*

This is another infilling of the Holy Spirit, another empowerment through speaking in tongues. Peter had gone to this prayer meeting from a situation where he was in trouble with the magistrates of that area because of helping someone and because of a healing that took place in the area. We're going to look at something else that took place after this, another experience of Peter's life as a result of and in relation to supernatural prayer.

Acts 5:12-16: *"And through the hands of the apostles many signs and wonders were done among the people. And they were all with one accord in Solomon's porch. Yet none of the rest dared join them but people esteemed them highly and believers were increasingly added to the Lord, multitudes of both men and women. So that they brought the sick out into the streets and laid them on beds and couches that at least the shadow of Peter passing by might fall on some of them. Also, a multitude gathered from the surrounding cities to Jerusalem bringing sick people and those that were tormented by unclean spirits and they were all healed."*

Peter was one of those that God was using dynamically as a result of supernatural prayer. The cause was supernatural prayer. The effect was supernatural power that was flowing mightily through this man called Peter. He didn't have to lay hands on anybody because the anointing flowed out of him if he got close enough for his shadow to even pass by them. So there was a supernatural release of power based upon a previous experience of supernatural prayer, praying in the spirit.

JESUS

John 11:28-37: *"And when she had said these things she went her way and secretly called Mary, her sister, saying, 'The teacher has come and* *is calling for you.' And as soon as she heard that she rose up quickly and came to Him. Now Jesus had not yet come into the town but was in the place that Martha met Him. Then the Jews who were with her in the House in comforting her when they saw that Mary rose up quickly and went out, followed her saying, 'She is going to the tomb to weep there.' Then, when Mary came to where Jesus was and saw Him she fell down at His feet and said, 'Lord if you had been here my brother would not have died.' Therefore when Jesus saw her weeping and the Jews who came with her weeping, <u>He groaned in the spirit</u> and was troubled. And He said, 'Where have you laid him?' They said, 'Lord come and see.' Jesus wept. Then the Jews said, 'See how He loved him.' And some of them said, 'Could not this man who opened the eyes of the blind also have kept this man from dying?' Then <u>Jesus again groaned in himself</u>, came to the tomb, and it was a cave and a stone lay against it."*

Jesus was facing a desperate situation. A very close friend of His had passed away and the other friends were very much troubled, grieving, hurting, crying. Jesus was feeling their pain, their hurt, so <u>He began to groan in the spirit</u>.

<u>*"He groaned in the Spirit . . ."*</u> is a very similar phrase to that which is found in Romans 8:26, *"Likewise the Spirit also helps our weakness, for we do not know not what we should pray for as we ought but the Spirit Himself makes intercession for us <u>with groanings which cannot be uttered."</u>* The same praying in the spirit that is spoken of in Romans 8 is also in John 11:28-44.

Twice Jesus groaned in the Spirit, or groaned in himself, in His spirit. These two things, that He groaned in the Spirit and He groaned in Himself, convey the same meaning.

The cause was He groaned in the Spirit. The effect was be a supernatural release of power.

John 11:39-44: *"Jesus said, 'Take away the stone.' Martha, the sister of him who was dead, said to Him, 'Lord, by this time there is a stench, for he has been dead four days.' Jesus said to her, 'Did I not say to you that if you believed that you would see the glory of God?' Then they took away the stone from the place where the dead man was lying and Jesus lifted up His eyes and said, 'Father, I thank you that you have heard Me and I know that you always hear me, but because of the people who are standing by I said this, that they may believe that you sent Me.' Now when He had said these things He cried with a loud voice, 'Lazarus, come forth.' And he who had died came out, bound hand and foot with grave clothes and his face was wrapped with a cloth. Jesus said to them, 'Loose him and let him go.'"*

<u>Jesus groaned in the Spirit twice, then released a supernatural flow of power that brought a man out of the grave, brought him back to life from the grave</u>. A supernatural release of supernatural power resulting from supernatural prayer.

I'm going to share an experience that happened in my life several years ago in a town in western Oklahoma. I was traveling back and forth each night at a special revival we held in western Ok. I was preaching in a church with 80 to 100 people attending each night. It took 30 minutes to an hour to get to the meeting from where I lived, so while I was driving I would pray in the spirit.

One particular evening while I was praying in the spirit I got caught up in a language that sounded like an African dialect. It just repeated over and over. It was like I was locked in to that particular prayer language. I wasn't deviating into another language, I was locked into a particular prayer language and a particular sound and syllables. As I prayed these syllables over and over, I did not know that there would be something powerful take place at the meeting just a few hours later.

As we entered the building, the praise and worship was excellent and great things were going on. I shared the message the Lord had given me and then I began to minister to people. I knew that something special was taking place inside of me.

I remember one lady who was coming toward the front to be prayed for. I was stretching out my hands as she was coming up toward the front and out of my spirit shot a power from God, a Holy Ghost anointing that came right up out of my spirit. It just shot out of me. And when it did, this power hit this lady, lifted her up in the air and set her on the front pew. When it did she raised both hands and began to weep and began to cry and began to praise God. She kept saying, *"Thank you Lord for healing me. Thank you Lord for setting me free."* God supernaturally touched her with a release of power.

As I began to walk up the aisle, I found myself about ten or fifteen feet away from four very large gentlemen. The one in the middle was about 6'6" and weighed about 380 lbs. He was a *very* big man. And there were three big men behind him getting ready to catch him because they knew what was going to happen. As I was just walking toward him, getting ready to lay hands on this man, another burst of power from my spirit shot out of me like a rocket of supernatural power. It looked like God was bowling that night and He bowled a strike. He rolled all four of those big men backwards on the floor. God supernaturally healed this man and not just him, but touched the other men who had been standing behind him. A supernatural release of power.

The Lord directed us to have a prayer line that night and in the prayer line, people began to get healed of all types of illnesses. All types of things were going on and I noticed that a whole family of Spanish-speaking people got in the prayer line. When it came their turn, I felt led to ask them, "What is it you have need of?" And with broken English, each one said, "We want Jesus." I knew that they were saying they wanted to be saved, so I led each one through the sinner's prayer to accept Jesus as their Lord and Savior. By the time the service was over, every family member from that Spanish speaking family was born again and Spirit filled.

A tremendous anointing of power was released through the cause and effect. The cause is supernatural prayer and the effect was a releasing of the supernatural power of God that was stored up while praying in the Holy Ghost.

Supernatural power is released through supernatural prayer.

THE GIFT THAT GROWS AND GROWS

Ezekiel 47:1 & 2: *"Afterward He brought me again to the door of the house. Behold waters issued out from under the threshold of the house eastward for the forefront of the house stood toward the East and the waters came down from under the right side of the house at the south side of the altar."*

This is a passage about the water that flowed from the very throne room of God. Water is a type of the Holy Spirit, a type of the fullness of the Spirit, a type of the anointing of the Spirit. Water is flowing from heaven, coming forth from the throne room of God.

Ezekiel 47:3: *"And when the man who had the line in his hand went forth Eastward he measured a thousand cubits and he brought me through the waters. The waters were to the ankles. Again he measured a thousand and he brought me through the waters. The waters were to the knees. Again he measured a thousand and he brought me through the waters. The waters were to the loins. Afterward he measured a thousand and it was a river that I could not pass over for the waters were risen, waters to swim in. A river that could not be passed over."*

There is no stopping place to what you can receive of anything that has to do with the Spirit of God. There is no attaining all that the Holy

Spirit has to offer. Throughout eternity, we are still going to be receiving things.

Paul talks about the unsearchable riches that are found in Christ. *"Christ"* means the anointed one and His anointing. No matter how much you learn about God, there is more to learn. In heaven, you will not know it all right away. About the time you think you know everything about God or everything about a certain aspect of God, He will reveal more and more to you.

There are basically five different areas you can grow in. You can grow in grace, knowledge, faith, experience and power.

THE GRACE OF GOD

We can grow in the grace of God, specifically in the grace of supernatural prayer.

2 Peter 3:18: *"But grow in grace and in the knowledge of our Lord and Savior, Jesus Christ, to whom be the glory both now and forever, Amen."*

The Greek word for *"grow"* is *"owxano."* It means to enlarge or to increase. God wants you to grow, to increase, to be enlarged, in the things of the Spirit. It is very important that we become fat and flourishing in the Spirit.

The word *"grace"* is a Greek word, *"kharece."* It means a divine influence upon the heart that is shown forth by the reflection upon the life. When God begins to move on your life, He first deals with your heart and then it is seen in your life. His grace is that which moves upon your life to literally bring a metamorphosis to your life to change you from what you have been into what you need to be.

When Paul said, *"By the grace of God, I am what I am."* he was saying, *"I have become what God wants me to be because of the grace of God."* Grace will cause you to be what God has called you to be and to do what God has called you to do. You are not able to do it by yourself.

Grace is God's influence on your heart that is reflected by a change in your life.

When someone comes to Jesus, there should be a tangible change in his life. He may still have some bondages in the natural, some problems he is trying to get rid of. But there will be an insatiable desire to get closer to God, a desire to serve God, a desire to be in the house of God, that was never there before. There will be a reflection in his life according to the divine influence upon the heart.

Grace is also described as God's riches at Christ's expense. For years, we thought it was totally unmerited, unearned. It is unmerited in the sense that it is God who initiates grace, not based on our righteousness or on our works. He initiates it. However, once I respond to grace, grace will be increased. Grace is increased through righteousness.

Romans 5:17-21: *"For if by one man's offense death reigned by one much more they which received an abundance of grace and of the gift of righteousness shall reign in life but one Jesus Christ. Therefore as by the offense of one judgement came upon all men to condemnation. Even so, by the righteousness of one, the free gift came upon all men unto justification of life. For as by one man's disobedience many were made sinners, by the obedience shall many be made righteous. Moreover the law entered that offense might abound. But where sin abounded grace did much more abound. That as sin hath reigned unto death, even so might grace reign through righteousness unto eternal life by Jesus Christ our Lord."*

The word, *"reign,"* simply means that it will be supreme, that it will take a place of authority. As I begin to walk in righteousness, grace will reign. As I begin to press in to have more prayer in my life, the grace of God will increase. The *"grace"* of God is the gifts of God, the goodness of God, the presence of God, the power of God . . . That is all grace. Salvation is grace. Have you ever noticed, the more you pray, the

more you will have the presence of God? The more you pray, the more grace begins to reign. The more you press into prayer, the more the gifts begin to flow. As you increase in righteousness, you increase in grace.
2 Peter 3:18: *"But grow in grace, and in the knowledge of our Lord and Saviour Jesus Christ."*

So, you can do something to increase the grace of God. The initiating of it is unmerited, but the increasing of it comes by what you do. Before you were saved, before you realized that God loves you He died for you. That was the unmerited grace of God. But, once you enter into grace, grace can abound and reign due to your actions.

We all need to get to the place that grace is reigning. When grace is reigning in your life, you will have great power in God, you will flow in the anointings of God, you will have great blessing upon your life.

So you can grow in grace by pressing into God through prayer in the Spirit, resulting in walking in righteousness. *"Righteousness"* means right standing with God, a position right next to God, right with God, right attitude, right actions, right lifestyle, that which is right . . . When you start walking in that which is right, righteousness, grace will come upon you and literally cover you with glory.

THE KNOWLEDGE OF GOD

The Greek word for *"knowledge"* is *"ghinoceko."* It means to understand, to perceive. We grow in our perception, our understanding of the Word of God.

Every time you pray in the Spirit, you grow in the knowledge of God. When you pray in the Spirit, you give the Holy Spirit the opportunity to teach you, to increase the knowledge of the Word. You become more sensitive to the Word every time you pray in the Spirit.

Smith Wigglesworth said that some people read the Word in the Greek, some in Hebrew, some in English. But, he said that he preferred to read the Word in the Holy Ghost. He said the Holy Spirit knows what the

Word means, and the Holy Spirit is our teacher. So he said he would pray in the Holy Spirit before, during and after reading the Bible. The Holy Spirit will bring the true understanding of the Word.

2 Peter 3:18: *"Grow in the grace and in the knowledge . . ."*

So, we can grow in the knowledge of God.

2 Peter 1:2: *"Grace and peace be multiplied unto you through the knowledge of God and of Jesus our Lord. . ."*

This scripture is telling us that grace and peace can be increased by increasing the knowledge of God. So, grace is not only increased through righteousness, it is also increased through knowledge.

Peter is not talking here about head knowledge. He uses that same Greek word, *"ghinoceko,"* which means to perceive, to understand. Only the Holy Spirit can give you that understanding. He wrote it, so He understands it.

As you begin to press into prayer in the Spirit, as you begin to have koinonea (fellowship), as you begin to have an intimate relationship with the Holy Spirit, He begins to share with you the knowledge of the Word.

2 Peter 1:3: *"According as His divine power has given unto us all things that pertain unto life and godliness through the knowledge of Him that hath called us by glory and virtue."*

Everything that I need in this world, that means the natural things that I need, and the things of godliness, the things I need of the Spirit, come from the knowledge of Jesus. And where does the knowledge of Jesus come from?

What happened to Peter in the 16th chapter of Matthew when Jesus asked, *"Whom do men say that I am?"* The disciples answered, *"Some say Elijah. Some say that you are a great prophet."* And Jesus asked, *"But, who do you say that I am?"* Peter answered, *"Thou art the Christ, the Son of the Living God."* Jesus said, *"Flesh and blood did not reveal this to you, only my Father in heaven."* And how does the Father reveal it? By His Spirit.

Revelation and understanding comes from the Spirit of God. If you try to understand the Word of God by yourself, with your own natural thinking, you will only come up with weird doctrines. That is why there are so many different churches and beliefs. The reason there are so many cult practices is that people mentally try to come to an understanding of the Word and have gone astray. Your natural thinking can never comprehend a full understanding of God's Word. True knowledge of God's Word only comes from a close relationship with the Spirit of God, cultivated through much prayer in the Spirit. Supernatural prayer results in supernatural knowledge of God's Word.

FAITH

Every time you pray in the Spirit, your faith grows. As you pray in the Spirit, you come into contact with Almighty God. Every time you pray in the Spirit, you come into direct contact with the Holy Spirit.

2 Thessalonians 1:3: *"We are bound to thank God always for you, brethren, as it is meet because that your faith groweth exceedingly. And that the charity of every one of you all toward one another abounds."*
Jude 20: *"Building up yourself on your most holy faith, praying in the Holy Ghost."*

While you pray in the Holy Spirit, you are building up your faith which has a foundation in Jesus Christ. When you hear the Word, faith comes. When you pray in the Spirit, you are building upon that faith which came by hearing the Word. So, if you want your faith to increase, pray more in tongues, in the Spirit. The more you pray in the Spirit, the more your faith will increase.

The word *"building"* has the connotation of charging up, increasing, building higher and higher. It is like putting together a building. The building contractor comes in with plans and begins building the foundation. After the foundation is built, he begins to put up the framework. Then he may begin to contract out the electric work and the plumbing and other things. Before long they are going to put the insulation in the walls. Then they put the sheet rock up and finish it. Then they go from there until the house is completed.

When you hear the Word the foundation is built. Then you begin to pray in the Spirit, you begin to build up of your spiritual house. The Word is the foundation and prayer in the Spirit is the building up of your spiritual skyscraper.

The word, *"faith"*, is the Greek word, *"pistis,"* meaning reliance, consistency, being fully persuaded, totally convinced. It is amazing that as you begin to pray in the Spirit, you become totally convinced of what the Word says. As you pray in the Spirit you become fully persuaded, you become consistent, constant, stable.

EXPERIENCE

First we must remember that an experience with God is not foundational. The Word is foundational and the experience is more like the appliances you put in your new house. They are important and they are necessary, but they are not the foundation. We must remember to build upon the rock. We must first have a solid foundation or the house will not stand for long.

Romans 5:1-4: *"Therefore being justified by faith we peace with God through our Lord, Jesus Christ, by whom also we have access by faith* *unto this grace wherein we stand and we rejoice in the hope of the glory of God. And not only so, but we glory in tribulation also, knowing that our tribulation worketh patience, and patience experience, and experience hope, and hope maketh not ashamed because the love of God is shed abroad in our hearts by the Holy Ghost which is given unto us."*

Faith is the computer code by which we have access to grace. We get into grace through faith.

Notice that this scripture does not say that tribulation gives us patience. It says that tribulation puts patience to work. Patience is a fruit of the Spirit, developed by prayer in the Spirit, by study of the Word and by righteousness. If patience came from trouble, we would have a very patient world. Think about it. How many times have you seen someone who is impatient, who is in trouble? How many impatient people do you know who have had a lot of trouble in life? Did all that trouble make them patient? Religion says that tribulation will give you patience but that is not what the Bible says. The Bible says that tribulation puts patience to work and that makes sense. According to Galatians 5, patience is one attribute of the fruits of the Holy Spirit. It comes from the Holy Spirit, not from trouble. Prayer in the Spirit builds up the fruits of the Spirit in our lives. The closer we get to the Holy Spirit, the more the fruit of patience will grow.

When you have gone through something patiently, believing that through faith and patience you inherit every promise, the end result will be that you will indeed receive the promise of God that you were patiently believing for. Let's say, for example that you are in need of a physical healing and you get into the Word and you believe for a healing, but the healing hasn't manifested yet. But you stay in the Spirit. You pray in the Spirit and you read the Word of God. You stand on scripture and you say, *"By His stripes I am healed. That means it is a done deal. It has already happened. I am healed, whether I feel like it or not."* So you begin to pray in the Spirit about that because you want to pray what God says, not what your body says. And the Spirit of God begins to bear witness with your spirit and lets you know that is true. The Holy Spirit makes that scripture more alive to you and you begin to realize that it is something you have to stand for until it manifests. You begin to realize that patience must go to work and having done all, you stand. You might have to stand and stand and stand, and patiently stand some more. Your patience must work. Then the day comes that what you are standing for begins to manifest. <u>Your patience has brought an experience in God.</u>

You have experienced what it was to stand in faith in the midst of circumstances that contradicted everything that the Word of God said. You have had an experience in God. So what happens the next time the enemy attacks you? You reply by saying, *"devil, we've been here before and I can and will outlast this storm. I know how to trust God and I know how to patiently weather the trouble until the blessing comes through."*

Experiences that are based upon the Word of God will strengthen you for your next season of attack. David, through faith and through the Word, slew a lion and a bear. When he came up against a bigger foe, he thought of his past experiences. He thought back to the time he slew the lion and to the time he slew the bear. And he said in 1 Samuel 17:34-36, *"Through the power of God, I slew the lion. Through the power of God, I slew the bear. And through the power of God I am going to slay this uncircumcised Philistine."* The experiences in God that he had before strengthened him for a bigger experience. We grow in experience. Later in his life he came against some bigger opponents and he drew on these former experiences to overcome them, also.

Some people try to take the experience and make it fit the Word of God. We need to take God's Word and have an experience based on God's Word. We need to take God's Word and have an experience from it. If we have an experience and then try to make God's Word fit the experience, we will wind up believing in twisted scriptures, in a false word. For example, when someone has cancer, there is always someone who will twist the scriptures and say, "Well, this is your burden to bear, this is your cross to carry, fall over and die." When we take our experience and try to find a scripture to fit our experience, to justify our experience, it breeds defeat. We need to take God's Word and then have an experience from the Word, out of the Word and because of the Word. Experience should come from the Word? On account of the Word and because of the Word. The Word first, experience second. It is not experience first and then try to find a scripture to fit it. That is out of order.

So we grow in our experiences. The Greek word for experience is *"dokeemay"* and it means to be tried, to be tested, and to have the mark of approval. It means do God's Word. His Word has been tried and tested before and has come forth as purest gold. Seven times. Put His Word to the ultimate test in your life and it will come out with the stamp of approval.

Psalms 34:8: *"O taste and see that the Lord is good. Blessed is the man that trusteth in Him."*

This scripture is telling us to have an experience and see that the Lord is good. You do that by praying in the Spirit and by the Holy Ghost you are able to drink of the Living Water.

John 7:37: *"In the last day, that great day of the feast, Jesus stood and cried saying, 'If any man thirst, let him come unto me and drink. He that believeth on me as the scripture hath said, out of his belly shall flow rivers of living water.' But this spake He of the Spirit which they that believe on Him should receive. For the Holy Ghost was not yet given because that Jesus was not yet glorified."*

Jesus was speaking here of the baptism of the Holy Spirit. He was saying that you've got to be thirsty, come and drink, partake of the Holy Spirit. Taste and see that the Lord is Good. Have an experience in God by praying in the Spirit.

There are two different types of experiences. There is the physical, soulish experience and there is the spiritual experience. Something has to happen in the spiritual first, which will later give you the physical experience. So the spiritual experience should be the one you look for the most. Then the physical experiences will come in due time. Many times, while I am praying in the Spirit, I simply sense the Lord's presence. I may sense that He is pleased or I may feel the peace of God come over me. I may have dreams or visions or I may just know that I know that God has heard my prayer. I may have other spiritual experiences, but that is all I need for the moment. I may not have felt anything in my flesh. But that does not mean that I won't. It may take a week or a month but that doesn't make it any less than a miracle. The devil wants you to get in the area of immediacy. He wants you to think that the answer to your prayer has to come immediately or it won't come at all. But there is a spiritual experience and then there is a physical experience. Sometimes when I pray I don't feel a thing. But some times when I pray it's like fire, I can feel that things are happening.

CONCLUSION

DON'T EVER QUIT

You should never give up. Never give out. Never give in. There is no stopping place.

1 Corinthians 9:24: *"Know ye not that they which run in a race run all. But one receives the prize so run that ye may obtain. And every man that striveth for the mastery is temperate in all things. Now that they do it to obtain a corruptible crown but we an incorruptible. I therefore so run not as uncertainty so fight I, not as one that beats the air. And I keep my body and bring it under subjection that less by any means that when I preach to others I myself should be a castaway."*

Don't ever quit. You obtain by never stopping. Don't stop running. Don't stop praying.

There is no stopping place.

Your body will be one of your biggest hindrances to the things of the Spirit. Your body will be tired. It will say, *"You need a vacation. You need a rest, today."* But this scripture says that if you obey your body, you will become a castaway. Paul said that if he didn't bring his body under subjection he would become a castaway. Even while he was preaching and others were getting blessed and getting saved, he wouldn't even make it.

Philippians 3:13 & 14: *"Brethren, I count not myself to have apprehended but this one thing I do; forgetting those things which are behind and reaching forth for those things which are before."*

Paul is saying here that he realizes that he has to forget the things of the past, both the good and the bad, in order to press into the future. It is very easy for us to look back into the past, even to look at the good things of the past, and to live in that and not press for a greater experience in God. It's so easy to think and say, *"Oh, God moved so beautifully, yesterday."* And it is so easy to live in those past experiences instead of pressing into future experiences of God. A good experience is actually an enemy to a better experience. And a better experience is an enemy to the best experience. If you live in the good memories of the past, they will hinder you from obtaining the better things that God has for you.

So, Paul said he would have to forget those things and press toward the mark for the prize of the high calling of God in Christ Jesus. He was saying, *"I'm not going to quit!! I've had some great experiences in the past, but I'm going to press in to some higher ones. I'm going for the prize."*

2 Timothy 4:7 & 8: ***"I have fought a good fight. I have finished my course. I have kept the faith. Henceforth there is laid up for me a crown of righteousness which the Lord the righteous judge shall give me on that day. Not to me only, but to all them that love his appearing."***

That means he didn't quit. He did not quit until it was done.

2 Timothy 4:5: *"I am now ready to be offered and the time of my departure is at hand."*

The only time to quit is when you go home to be with Jesus. We can't quit fighting until we get to heaven. We can lay down our cross, lay down our crown, lay down our armor when we get to the other side. We won't need those things when we get to heaven.

Keep praying in the Spirit. Keep pressing into the Spirit. Keep on keeping on. The gifts of the Spirit and supernatural prayer will grow and grow as long as you press in. For as long as you live there is more for you to know about prayer, and prayer in the Spirit. There is more to know about the supernatural of God. There are more experiences to have. You must keep pressing in and never quit until you get to the other side.

- Discernment by faith
- is a person
- Through tongues that have been tested

PRAY WHAT you
DON'T KNOW
SO THAT
YOU MAY KNOW
unknown to known
— to positive

Made in the USA
Lexington, KY
23 November 2012